I0623441

# MY TRAVEL MEMOIR

### BY
## SYLVIA X. ZHANG

**My Travel Memoir**

**Author:** Sylvia X. Zhang

**Paperback ISBN:** 979-8-9914012-0-3
**eBook ISBN:** 979-8-9914012-1-0

**Publication Date:** September 1, 2024

Library of Congress Control Number: 2024917620

**Published and Distributed by:**
**Asian Culture Press LLC**
1942 Broadway St., Suite 314c,
Boulder, CO 80302,
United States

**Cover Photo Credit:** Sophia YK Sun and Sylvia X. Zhang
**Editor:** Allan K. A. Marson

© 2024 by Sylvia X. Zhang. All rights reserved. No part of this book may be reproduced, stored in a retrieval system, or transmitted in any form or by any means, electronic, mechanical, photocopying, recording, or otherwise, without the prior written permission of the publisher.

For information about permission to reproduce selections from this book, write to Asian Culture Press LLC, 1942 Broadway St., Suite 314c, Boulder, CO 80302, United States.

This is a work of nonfiction. Names, characters, places, and incidents are either the product of the author's imagination or used fictitiously. Any resemblance to actual events, locales, or persons, living or dead, is entirely coincidental.

Printed in the United States of America.

*To Mom*

# Preface

I love memories. They don't contradict my belief in "Living in the Moment." Memories are very important to who I am now.

During the difficult times of the pandemic and my daughter's puberty, I yearned to walk on the wooden paths of Mount Hua, listening to and feeling the wind in the valley. Without delay, I bought train tickets and booked a hotel for myself, but I couldn't go due to the sudden lockdown in that area. I was in urgent need of an escape, so I started to recall and write down my trips.

Traveling is my source of energy. When I travel, I am myself, not a mom, daughter, wife, or lawyer. I wish I could be who I truly am.

Sylvia

July 25, 2024

# CONTENTS

*Contents*

*My Travel Memoir*

*Contents*

# I

# Early Years' Travel with Mom

I bet my mom loved traveling as I do, though I never had a chance to ask her. There are several old photo albums at home with faded or black and white photos of trips, where I can see my pretty mom smiling gracefully at the beach or temples or foothills, with or without the skinny boyish me beside her.

Mom was always complacent about going back to work at the library of the college she had graduated from after leaving the military, so she could have winter and summer vacations to be my companion, staying at home or taking short-distance trips. I started traveling around and outside Beijing as early as my primary school years in the mid-1980s, and had been to the seaside twice during my middle school years when I happened to grow taller than average and beyond any expectation. Later we tended to "blame" my extraordinary height (1.8 meters or 5.9 feet) on the great deal of calcium intake from the seafood I ate at that time, such as small crabs and other shellfish.

One summer when I was nine, we went to visit our extended family in Qinhuangdao, Hebei Province, a nice, clean coastal city 300 kilometers east of Beijing. Both Mom and I liked the city very much and we even talked about moving there from Beijing. Then came a stormy night when the loud and most horrible cracking of the thunder scared us to death. We immediately gave up any idea about relocating. I, for the first time in my life, began to feel homesick.

Mom and I started our trips to the suburban areas of Beijing as early as the 1990s when Beijing countryside tours were not popular and public transportation was quite inconvenient. One summer we got up very early when it was dark outside and took two buses to Dongzhimen

Long-Distance Bus Station to catch a special bus heading to Miyun County (now Miyun District), northeast of Beijing and surrounded by the Yanshan Mountains and Miyun Reservoir. After a nearly two-hour drive, we reached the Miyun County Bus Station where Mom bargained for a private minivan to take us on a half-day tour at Miyun at RMB 40 yuan. The taxi drove us at first to the Black Dragon Pond and waited outside that scenic spot for us to see the ponds and waterfalls and have our picnic lunch. Then we came back to the taxi for our next stop, the Top Waterfall of Beijing, and went for about one hour's walk. Lastly, we went to Elf Valley for a quick hike and took the minivan back to Miyun Bus Station to catch the last bus back to town. The schedule was a bit tight and tiring, like the currently trendy "soldiers' field exercise", but we managed to enjoy the rich natural environment of waterfalls and ponds, mountains and valleys within one day at a reasonable cost. I became so used to tight travel schedules and a limited budget that even now when I can afford better travel conditions and have more available time, I am still a thrifty traveler.

One summer during middle school, we took a boat trip.

Mom and I took the train to Tianjin and got on board a huge ship heading to Yantai, Shandong Province to visit her friend. Mom had been thrifty all her life, especially when I was little. She bought us the cheapest fourth-class tickets, so we had to stay almost at the bottom of the ship, sleeping on bunk beds in a crowded, poorly ventilated area. We became seriously seasick at night because of the intense sea waves and terrible smell, and had to stay up quite late sitting on the deck to recover.

Another trip to Shandong Province was more pleasant. During the National Holiday of my first year of university, we took a train to Qufu, the hometown of Confucius, and began without delay to climb Mount Tai in the late afternoon. When we finally arrived at the landmark mountain top, the Southern Heavenly Gate (Nan Tian Men), it was almost midnight and we were exhausted. Mom found a cheap hotel with some bunk beds and a large bed for a couple of people so that we could take a nap for a few hours before going out to see the amazing sunrise on Mount Tai. When we made our way down the mountain later that day, Mom took a photo of me leaning on the granite stone in front of the "Kong Zi Deng Lin

Chu", the place where Confucius climbed the mountain. More than twenty years later when Mom has long gone, I went to Mount Tai again with my own family, watching the sunrise and taking a photo of me leaning on the same granite stone, with my lovely daughter standing on the other side.

After the trip to Mount Tai, Mom and I took a couple of self-guided trips in suburban Beijing and nearby provinces during the holidays. Once we took the train to escape from the summer heat in Beijing and visited the Imperial Mountain Resort and some temples in Chengde, Hebei Province. I became obsessed with mountains and hills and would even climb the rocks inside the royal garden in my sandals. I also had my first horse riding experience in the Empire Qing's summer palace.

We also joined a group tour to Shaanxi Province. We first visited the famous Emperor Qin's Terracotta Warriors and spent RMB 180 yuan (quite a lot of money for my family in the late 1990s) on buying a brochure, as it was a great honor to have the autography of the farmer who initially found these historical remains. The tour guide urged us to buy the signed brochure because the farmer was illiterate except for being able to sign his own name, and on the day of our visit he happened to be at the place. However, it turned out that he was basically at the place every day.

Then we went on to our next stop, Mount Hua, the most remarkable mountain I have ever visited. I hold this opinion even today after placing my footprints on quite a lot of amazing mountains and hills around the world. I was totally immersed in the rocky and precipitous mountains and was not at all afraid of the heights and cliffs. I went to all four peaks while my mom went up one with me and then waited for me at the North Peak in the middle area.

The cliffside path at the West Peak was the most dangerous and thrilling. I walked steadily and calmly on the crude wood panels driven into the vertical cliff while holding in one hand the iron chains nailed into the cliff and grabbing my camera and water bottle in the other hand. A few years later after more and more accidents happened, visitors were required to be equipped with safety belts. A boy older than me in our tour group was too scared to continue the plank walk, when he retreated and held the iron chains tightly with both hands, I had to surpass him by inclining my body towards the abyss-like valley. I really long to see that stunning mountain view again sometime in the future and even wish to have half of my ashes poured out there after I die.

Like other group tours, we had a fixed schedule that didn't leave much time for me to enjoy the lush pines and fresh air in the serene mountains and valleys. Since I was the only one in the group exploring the West Peak and walked much faster than the others, my mom decided to take the cable car down the mountain first and left my ticket at the cable car station, but required that anyone picking up the ticket must write down my name correctly. Not until I had run all the way back to find my mom at the cable car station and heard my name "Student xx from Beijing" broadcast from the speaker, did I realize that my mom left my ticket there. I went to the staff and wrote down my name on the back of the ticket as requested. They seemed quite satisfied, saying that, "your mom is really smart, telling us that you are easy to identify because you are such a tall girl and your first name is a difficult Chinese character, so no imposter could pick up your ticket." I laughed too and was even happier to be able to cut in the crowded waiting line, guided by the staff, and finally catch up just in time with my mom and the tour group.

# II

# Travel with Classmates during University

I made a couple of trips with my classmates when I was in college, two of which were with my female high school classmate and her male classmates in Tsinghua University. We went to see the well-known ice and snow sculptures in Harbin, Heilongjiang Province during one winter vacation and went skiing at Yabuli, a small village at that time and currently an international ski resort. That was my first time going back to see my birthplace in Harbin, where I had stayed for about 3 months after my birth before being taken to Beijing. A taxi driver said I looked like a typical northeastern girl with a large stature, a large face and large eyes. Nevertheless, I was obviously not typical enough to handle the cold of the Northeast Chinese winter. Although I was wearing my heaviest and longest coat, equipped with knitted scarf and cap and two pairs of gloves, I was still shivering outdoors.

During another summer vacation, I went with the same girl and her pals to Dandong, the hometown of one of the boys, a border city of east Liaoning Province, where we lingered on the broken bridge crossing over the Yalu River and overlooked the desolate landscape in North Korea/the DPRK. We hiked a local mountain called Phoenix Mountain and cooled down splashing each other in a stream next to a part of the Great Wall built in Ming Dynasty. It was unforgettable to watch the sunrise at the early hour of four o'clock in the morning and I deeply appreciate the delicious fried seafood the boy's mom cooked for us in her small, hot kitchen.

Another trip to Shanxi Province with my own university classmate (a boy) came about by chance. I had no idea about the gossip about his relationship with another girl in my class (it turned out to be fruitless), so when I knew he was planning a journey to the Yungang Grottoes, Hanging Temple and Mount Wutai during the National Holiday and there was an extra train ticket, I took it without hesitation or embarrassment.

In addition to the fluent BBC-accented English he displayed in class, my travel companion turned out to be very knowledgeable. Although we were unfamiliar with each other and it was a bit awkward in the beginning, the trip was fine. The funniest part was when we came out of the Yungang Grottoes and waited for a bus in the street. Our faces, clothes and backpacks were covered with coal ashes, as Datong, the so-called "China's coal capital", was famous for its coal mining industry and there were many coal trucks passing by at that time. Later we shared a jeep bound to Mount Wutai and the capital city Taiyuan with two older girls and one boy, who were co-workers in a foreign company at Guomao, the fancy office buildings of the International Trade Center in Beijing. The trip became more interesting as our new friends were quite sophisticated and humorous, sometimes mingled their conversation with pleasant English words. I enjoyed very much talking to them and could see my classmate did too. I started to yearn to work for a foreign invested company instead of working in a government institute or studying overseas after graduation.

My college graduation trip was a three-day event at a beach county about 250km east of Beijing, named Laoting, in Hebei Province. Almost all my classmates made it to the get-together. We swam in the sea, sang karaoke and drove off-the-road jeeps on the remote island. It was sad to say goodbye to the classmates after four years; a desolate beach at the undeveloped county of Laoting was an ideal place to shed farewell tears. We drank a lot of beer and took many photos together, wishing each other a promising future.

# III

# Travels with Tour Groups

## 1. Hainan

My first "solo" trip was made with a tour group to Hainan Province at the end of the year that I graduated from university. I began to work for an international accounting firm the second day after my graduation. The workload was pretty heavy and I worked really hard. By the year end I had accumulated quite a lot of overtime leave plus my pro-rated annual leave. I felt exhausted from work and studies for both the certified public accountant and legal qualification exams, and decided to take a luxury vacation as a reward.

My mom was not retired at that time and my annual leave could not be carried to the next year, so I had to travel alone, and I was totally fine with that. Group tours were very popular those years because of their well-arranged routes and cheap price for air tickets, meals and accommodation. I was the only single traveler in the group, so for most of the time I could enjoy a double room by myself without having to pay an extra price. We went to famous tourist spots in Haikou and Sanya as well as some other small cities like Xinglong and Wenchang. I tried Wenchang chicken, the chili yellow pepper sauce, freshly picked up coconut juice and had some delicious vegetarian cuisines at Nanshan Temple. I also watched the transgender show with the group and paid an extra fee to experience scuba diving in the dark and chilly sea water where my finger got nipped by some tiny yellow fish. I remember myself walking on the sand beach at the most southern point of Hainan Island with two giant boulders engraved with Chinese characters of "Tian Ya" and "Hai Jiao" (both mean "end of the Earth") situated on the beach, wearing my purple winter jacket and white capris after I caught a cold from the diving. The trip was a bit lonely but basically nice.

## 2. "Xin, Ma, Tai"

My first overseas trip, like many Chinese, was with a tour group heading to Singapore, Malaysia and Thailand around Christmas of my second year at work. The classic three neighboring countries were the first to open to Chinese tourists, and interestingly, the first characters of their Chinese names pronounce the same as those of three local places in Beijing – Xin Jie Kou, Ma Dian and Tai Ping Zhuang. I went with two co-workers from my firm, one woman two years older than me and one man my age.

The trip was tightly scheduled as always and barely made any impression on me until we would visit the famous Genting Casino in Malaysia. It turned out that the middle-aged man sharing the room with my male colleague traveled with the tour group for the sole purpose of gambling at Genting! We had indeed found him a bit eccentric because he traveled alone with little interest in visiting scenic spots along the route. As disclosed by my colleague as an "insider", the guy had taken a taxi to the casino the previous night, ahead of our schedule, won about RMB 2000 yuan and then come back to our hotel in the early morning. When we had our day tour to the casino, he slept at the hotel and went to play alone at night. He told my colleague the reason why he chose to come with the group was that the total cost for the tour was even less than his own expenditure on flights, meals and accommodation here. He had gambled for four nights at Genting with some winnings and losses, but overall had some winnings (without disclosing the exact amount to my colleague).

It seemed that our friend shared some luck with his roommate and won quite a lot of coins when playing the slot machines. I set a 100yuan limit on my play at the slot machines (the only game I dared to try) and lost my coins very quickly; so did my female colleague. When we found our male colleague won a full cup of coins from one shot, we were a bit envious and asked him to share some with us so we could play more. He smirked a few times before walking around, going to exchange the coins into paper bills, and not playing anymore! The female colleague had a sharp tongue and taunted the male colleague about his stinginess for a long time even after the trip.

## 3. Thailand and Sichuan

I had another two tour-group trips with my high school girlfriends. First, we four young women went to Thailand at the time of Songkran (water-splashing) Festival. On my previous trip to Thailand with my colleagues, I had watched the iconic transgender show, but I was too shy to express any interest or feeling. When I was with my high school girlfriends, I felt free to be myself and we enjoyed not only the show, taking many photos with the stunning half-naked performers, but also paid extra fees to watch the nude guys' show, which was a bit embarrassing but rebellious for young ladies. In the tour group, there were some young guys from a local tax bureau in Beijing about our age. We played water splashing intensely and the two guys seemed to have crushes on two of my girlfriends.

Later, in the year when I changed my job from the accounting firm to a legal consulting company, one of my girlfriends was studying overseas, and the other three of us went to Sichuan Province during the National Holiday. That was my first and only time to visit Jiuzhaigou and Huanglong. Before long the places went viral and are now constantly crowded. I can still remember how I was fascinated by the turquoise and teal-colored lakes surrounded by serene autumn woods. Going up the Huanglong Mountain was quite an effort. We had no experience with high altitude sickness at that time, so when we ran down the mountain to catch up with our group, we didn't realize that the headaches we felt were actually due to our running and jumping at 4000 meters above sea level.

A trivia about the Sichuang trip was that we were eager to see wild monkeys on Mount Emei, but we only met one large monkey during our three-hour walk on the mountain. Everyone was trying to feed it and the monkey was rather picky about food, like a king sitting proud and waiting to be served.

# IV

# Trips with Jeff

## 1. Backpacking Trips

I met my husband at my first job when we were working for the same accounting firm. We were both young and loved backpacking.

Our first trip was to Hangzhou and Suzhou and surrounding places in the early Spring of the year after our relationship had just started. Since our work was quite similar, we had to ask for annual leave for the same days which caused a lot of trouble including overtime work before and after our vacations, and questions and demands from our managers. We went anyway, together with another female colleague at a lower level in the office who had college classmates working in Hangzhou and arranged the tour for the three of us.

We went to many places such as the West Lake, Cold Mountain Temple, Xitang Watertown, Turtle Head Isle in Wuxi and so on. My best experience was to have green tea and snacks in a tea house next to the West Lake while enjoying the picturesque spring scenery in the southern regions of the Yangtze River. Jeff and I had our first quarrel about the ticket price when we planned to take a boat trip to Plum Blossom Island on Lake Taihu. I was quite thrifty, following my mom's example, and bargained over the tickets to get the price to the lowest point, while Jeff was more generous and believed that travel costs are supposed to contribute to the local economy so we shouldn't be so sensitive about money. The fight ended up with my victory, but we soon reconciled and gained a better understanding of each other's personality; people always say that new couples should travel together.

A funny incident during that trip was about a dish called "drunken shrimp" we had for dinner in Wuxi, Jiangsu

Province. The shrimp was relaxed but still alive after being submerged in strong Chinese rice wine in order to keep their freshness when caught daily from the lake. We three had been staring at the plate for quite some time before either of us decided to try one. When I was peeling off the shrimp shell, it moved a bit and I was so horrified that I immediately threw it back to the plate. Jeff also spit out the half-chewed shrimp and said it also moved inside his mouth. We felt horrified and couldn't stand chewing the shrimp alive and insisted the chef cook them for us in spite of laughter and persuasion from the waiters and chefs.

Since then, Jeff and I have continued to make a couple of backpack trips every year before and after getting married, in addition to my days off for study and exams and occasional journeys with my friends and my mom.

During the spring of 2003 before SARS came, we went to Shandong Province. We walked on the quiet beach and park lawns of Rizhao, climbed to the top of Mount Laoshan and even bought a wooden-framed kite in the capital of kites, Weifang. Our favorite place in Shandong was Qingdao. We liked this clean coastal city for its red-roofed German style villas, giant phoenix trees, affordable tasty seafood and beautiful sea views.

In April 2004, we flew to Kunming, Yunnan Province and took the sleeper bus to Dali. We arrived at the old town of Dali in the early morning and asked for an empty room at a hostel to wash our filthy faces and change our crumpled clothes before going to Mount Cangshan and Lake Erhai for a one-day tour. On the next day we went to the Old Town of Lijiang established in the Ming Dynasty with well-preserved ancient waterways, during daytime immersing ourselves in the hustle-bustle shopping street filled with exquisite Naxi Ethnic Minority cultural products with Dongba scripts and enjoyed the quiet evening in this "plateau water town".

On our way to the Jade Dragon Snow Mountain, our taxi driver recommended us to stop by a Buddhist temple. Jeff and I were separated for the tour in the main hall. The monk guiding my tour suggested that I light some blessing candles for family and friends at only RMB 2 yuan for each candle. I heard him mumbling that the candle should last at least for 49 (7 squared) or 81 (9 squared) days for better blessings, etc., and asked him if I could pay only 2 yuan for one candle lighting for one day. When he seemed reluctant to give an affirmative or negative answer, I brooded over the multiplication, felt uneasy and immediately left the hall. When I turned around to see the monk that was Jeff's guide pointing at the candles and talking to him, I realized that Jeff might not think through the situation before agreeing to light candles. I dared not talk loud about a trick that I was not 100% sure about, so I shouted to Jeff in English, "Jeff, you have to pay before lighting the candles!" In fact, my oral English at that time was not good enough to express my thoughts freely, but luckily Jeff felt the urgency and anxiety in my voice and came out right away. I whispered to him about my concern as to the number of days the candle would last for, and that the monks may insist that he pay the full price instead of just 2 yuan each. We both felt quite uncomfortable, and demanded the driver to take us straight to the destination.

Back in Kunming, we took the public mini-bus to the Shilin Stone Forest but it stopped by some tacky shops several times on the way. We were quite annoyed but the driver retorted that such detours were why the mini-bus tour cost only 20 yuan per person. Otherwise, we could spend over 200 yuan hiring a private car. We would in no way spend so much and had to give in. At that time, I noticed a foreign lady sitting on the backseat reading a book all the time while we had to get off the mini-bus at the stores. I felt both impressed about her calmness and embarrassed about the ridiculous transportation arrangement, and I hoped there would be more choices of affordable transportation for individual travelers in the future.

Generally speaking, our trip to Yunnan was very pleasant. Coming back from the top of the magnificent snow mountain, Jade Dragon, we went on a two-day tour to Lugu Lake and took a boat on the sapphire-like glistening lake in the morning sun. Due to our limited time and budget, we followed a preset tight schedule, took advantage of nighttime transportation and overcame the discomfort and sleepiness, stayed in primitive hostels and ate affordable local food in order to see as much scenery as possible.

We were surprised when we checked in for the return flight. The tickets had been actually oversold and our original seats were taken by others. However, since we booked the tickets much earlier than the others, the airline counter staff upgraded us to two business-class seats. We were in our wrinkled dirty jeans after a whole week's travel, surrounded by business travelers with suits and ties. Enjoying the drinks in glasses and food in porcelain plates instead of being served with disposable tableware, we felt really lucky.

During the Chinese Spring Festival of 2005, we were supposed to take an early flight to Nanjing, Jiangsu Province for a visit to Jeff's grandpa, but we got up late and missed our plane. We had to sign in and wait to see if there was any vacant seat on other flights bound to Nanjing later that day. We checked with the staff at the airline counter from time to time and found a guy with gold-rimmed glasses in a suit standing in front of the counter, occupying the best place to talk to the staff all the time. We politely asked him to move aside so that we could converse with the staff but he ignored us. After several times of failed requests, I could not help but cursing in a low voice. The guy heard it and turned around to yell at me. We started to quarrel, and very soon Jeff and the guy pushed each other and dropped their bags on the ground for a potential fist-fight. I stood between them trying to reason with the guy and suddenly got pushed by him down to the floor. I stood up with the airline staff's help and furiously kicked the guy in his stomach with my right foot. Some airline staff and people around us came over to separate us and the staff at the counter urged us to get ready to check in for the available seats. To my disappointment, the guy was also on board when we entered into the cabin of the plane.

In September 2005, we took a night train to the Yellow Mountains in Anhui Province, climbed from morning to dusk all the way up, slept in a nice but quite affordable hotel on top and on the second day hiked all the way down to Bright Summit (Guang Ming Ding), Lotus Peak (Lianhua Feng) and Heavenly Capital Peak (Tiandu Feng), as well as Guest-Greeting Pine (Yingkesong). That was the first time we finished such a challenging trek, which made us realize that, despite our (both of us happened to have) poor physical exam scores back in school, we were able to be persistent enough to complete the challenging walk. I still vividly remember that our legs were really sore, and we could barely bend our knees or walk freely up and down any stairs at the second stop of our trip, Thousand Island Lake.

We flew to Guangxi Province in the late fall of 2006. The Lijiang River cruise from Guilin to Yangshuo was a must-do but as soon as the huge ship set out, it couldn't get out of the port area for about an hour. The weather was a bit overcast, so the karst hills and mountains on the way seemed not very appealing. After we arrived at Yangshuo, we fell in love right away with the place where we enjoyed tasty food and drinks in the bourgeois-style bars and restaurants in West Street, went bamboo rafting along the meandering rivers surrounded by breathtaking rural scenery, and rode rented bikes tirelessly along bumpy ridges through lush green rice paddy fields and sugarcane farms.

The Yangshuo night show "Impression Liu Sanjie" directed by Zhang Yimou was famous for being China's first large natural environment theater show. In order to save a couple of hundred yuan we bought two 50-yuan tickets from the hostel owner. We, together with some other tourists, were taken secretly to a patch of bamboo forest in the darkness and seated on plastic stools. Since we were hidden behind the bamboos far away from the left side of the landscape stage, we could barely see the dancing show or hear clearly the folk songs. Jeff and I admitted that we made a huge mistake and would never be so stingy again when it comes to something worthwhile.

In the summer of 2007, we made a trip to Guizhou Province with two female friends, one of whom was my high-school classmate and fellow traveler from the Thailand and Sichuan trip, and the other one was her friend. There are many benefits to travel with friends, such as cost sharing for hostel rooms and private cars with local drivers (there were no rental cars available for driving at that time), trying more varieties of local food, not to mention having more fun together. We were deeply impressed by the turquoise colored lakes under the Large Seven-Hole Bridge and various waterfalls and ponds at the Seven Small Arches at Libo County, south of Guizhou Province, which could compete with the renowned lakes at Jiuzhaigou and Huanglong.

Qingyan Ancient Town was rather commercialized after gaining popularity for being the place where director Jiang Wen shot his black humor movie the Missing Gun. We had a feast in a pretty garden restaurant to celebrate Jeff's birthday.

We had planned to go rafting on the Maling River, famous for its thrilling experience, but were told that rafting was temporarily shut down due to a recent accident (thrilling indeed). It was a shame, but we continued our visit to the forests and lakes in the nearby Ten-Thousand Forest (Wanfenglin) Scenic Area, and were quite amazed by the numerous karst formations at Xingyi, Guizhou Province. On the way back to Guiyang, we managed to go rafting on the torrential river nearby Yellow Fruit Tree (Huangguoshu) Waterfall and had a lot of fun when we got soaking wet sitting in a rubber boat hitting the wild rapids in the white water. Most of all, however, neither of us could forget the tasty Guizhou sour-soup fish hotpot, and we looked for the same flavor for a long time after coming back to Beijing.

By October 2007, I had passed my legal qualification exam. Moreover, Jeff and I had paid off the mortgage loans for our first apartment. We decided to take a celebration trip to Dalian, Liaoning Province and do it in a luxurious way. We stayed at a four-star hotel, had afternoon coffee and tea, ordered seafood and other meals without much consideration of the price, and took taxies throughout our entire trip. The ironic part about this "extravagant" trip was that Jeff and I had taken separate airlines from Beijing to Dalian so that my flight ticket could be redeemed with accumulated miles. Our friends joked about our "separate trips" and my shrewdness. Although both of us felt uneasy about our extravagant spending in Dalian, we did have a great time doing the city walk and watching ocean park shows.

## 2. Hong Kong

Most of my early journeys to the "outside world" were made to Hong Kong. After working at the accounting firm for a couple of years, both Jeff and I joined an American law firm with its Asian headquarters located in Hong Kong, where our annual meetings and trainings were mostly held during the Christmas season. There were two memorable occasions during those trips:

One was an evening when Jeff and I were sitting on a bench in a public garden at the foot of Mount Tai Ping after taking the steepest cable cars we ever experienced going downwards. We were not alone; our colleagues were sitting nearby and intentionally leaving space for us to enjoy the quiet night. I was staring at the starry sky and kept silent for a while before suddenly shouting "Yes! I know it!" Jeff and our colleagues were all startled and curious, and I told them that I had been calculating the prices and payments I just made in one Sasa cosmetics shop on top of the mountain and couldn't reconcile them with my balance amount. All of them laughed out loud and were impressed with my obsession with money that successfully ruined the romantic vibe.

In fact, I was wronged by those guys (my colleagues were all guys) for making a fuss about money since it was not my own money. I was such a saver and I wouldn't spend money on anything unnecessary. I was actually on a "great" mission shopping for a full list of foreign brand cosmetics at Sasa for my friends and colleagues who didn't have a chance to visit Hong Kong, especially for those young and stylish secretaries working for the "upstairs lawyers".

Although having worked for more than two years, I was still like a "rookie" with student looks and mindset, and did not blend in with the fancy office buildings at Guomao where many luxury fashion stores were located. I had rarely used any high-end cosmetics sold in shopping malls in Beijing but they were cheaper in Hong Kong due to duty free policies, especially in the chain stores of Sasa. We Mainlanders would rush into one Sasa to present our shopping list to the BAs (beauty advisors) to locate the cosmetics we wanted and then made our payments straight away. If some cosmetics on the list could not be found, we would rush into another store because there were many Sasa stores in Hong Kong, e.g. two or three in one street. At the end of the trip, the names on the shopping list were cleared out, the money prepaid by friends and colleagues was paid up, and my luggage was full of fancy bottles as well as some (not all, not so greedy) free samples and gifts from BAs for myself.

Another special moment was hiking with Jeff and other colleagues on Lamma (Nan Ya) Island. The details about the hiking trip were rather vague; all I remember was that on a warm winter day, we meandered along the quiet alleys, beach and mountain trails on the island, whose name was mentioned in many Hong Kong drama shows I loved to watch at that time. I was wearing some Banelo or Bossini (frugal casual clothes brands of the late 1990s) long-sleeve T-shirts and a cross-body bag. That was one of my happiest hiking memories.

## 3. Maldives

The Maldives is a dream place for everyone yearning for a bright blue sky and crystalline seawater. It was the first foreign country I had visited without being with a tour group, and it was my honeymoon destination.

During the New Year Holiday after getting married on Christmas Day, Jeff and I joined a trip to Harbin with his elder brother as well as the latter's friends, including my future sister-in-law. We went to watch the ice sculptures during the evening at minus 20 degrees Celsius and our cameras stopped working, my future sister-in-law even had a serious stomachache. Later we went to ski at Yabuli where I kept falling down so heavily that I began to loathe skiing. I definitely wouldn't call that my honeymoon trip.

On my birthday in January 2004, Jeff and I set off for our five-day trip to the Maldives. We flew for about five hours to reach Colombo in Sri Lanka at midnight, where we transited to Male, the capital city of the Maldives. Then we took a speed boat for 40 minutes in darkness to arrive at Paradise Island at about 4 o'clock in the morning. Though exhausted, I was immediately fascinated by the transparent seawater below the floating bridge I stepped onto after getting off the boat.

Despite the lengthy travel time, we stayed for three full days on the island and it was like living in a real paradise. The sunny blue skies dotted with white cotton-candy clouds, the crystal clear greenish blue ocean water full of large and small colorful fish, the pretty cream flowers of pagoda trees and hibiscus, other tropical flowers, the sparkling swimming pools and various tropical foods, all left us with such an enjoyable and incredible memory.

Speaking of food, I had heard about the restaurants on the Maldives' islands were known for their high prices, so I booked a hotel with a whole-day buffet, including brunch and dinner, so that we didn't have to pay extra fees for food. We even brought two large bottles of mineral water in our luggage in case the bottled water sold on the island was too expensive (it turned out to be fairly priced). Many Chinese tourists would carry water and instant noodles and have all their meals in their rooms, which caused many complaints from Maldives hotels and waiters due to less income and more cleaning work. We decided not to act like stereotypical Chinese tourists nor leave any impression of being stingy, so we didn't use umbrellas and enjoyed getting a suntan on the beach and reading books by the swimming pools like Americans/Europeans did, and we ate all our meals at restaurants, ordered drinks not included in our buffet, and paid tips to the waiters.

Both of us got tanned and a bit burned but we didn't regret it a bit. I was wearing my first orange flora bikini and we went snorkeling with our own kits and saw a lot of colorful fish. The waiters treated us respectfully and chatted with us. I made up my mind to travel to at least one ocean island each year.

On our way back, our flight from Colombo to Beijing was delayed due to a heavy snow in Tokyo which affected our plane. We were taken to a five-star hotel in downtown Colombo and even had a half-day city walk, seeing some Hindu temples, a ruby store, the neat beach, and the slums next to the fancy hotel. On the plane back to Beijing later that night, I began to get accustomed to the hours-long flight and enjoyed the meals, naps and movies on the plane.

## 4. Australia

With the experience of our self-service trip to the Maldives, we planned a more complicated journey to east Australia in March 2007, for which Jeff had done a lot of research and reservations. We flew to Melbourne and went for a one-day bus tour with other tourists (mostly local seniors) to the Great Ocean Road, amazed by the quiet seaside towns, endless coastline views and magnificent giant boulders standing in the sea, the "12 Apostles". We were surprised to see a seventy-year-old grandpa taking a helicopter ride over the "12 Apostles" and hoped we would have the money and guts to take a helicopter ride someday in the near future.

We chose a tour package with a morning tea and bought our own lunch and supper on the way. Since the Australian accent was really different from American English we usually heard, ordering food was not easy. We went to a Subway restaurant for sandwiches the first day we arrived and were totally confused when being asked to choose the types of bread, sauce and vegetables. Jeff felt a bit awkward but I was shameless; I asked again and again making sure we got what we wanted. Because of this, I became the one to take care of our meals in foreign countries, which was vital to backpackers like us in order to have enough energy, save money, and taste more varieties of local food.

As for backpacks, apart from the knapsacks we each carried, we only brought one cabin-sized suitcase for our washbag and winter jackets as we had flown from the winter in Beijing to the summer in Australia. The customs official at the Melbourne airport was rather astonished that we only had such a small amount of luggage for a two-week trip. It turned out that each time when we checked out of our hotels, we did have problems packing due to buying more and more souvenirs, and I had to sit on the suitcase in order to zip it up.

After wandering in the Melbourne Zoo for a day where we got to know the ostrich-like emus and cute wombats, and took pictures of ourselves holding a heavy koala, we continued to fly north to Brisbane. The Surfers Paradise seemed unsuitable for swimming or snorkeling due to its sandy wind and strong waves, but we were busy and satisfied with our first-time stay at a nice rented apartment, where we could cook meals and live a life like the locals.

My deepest memory of Brisbane was its Dreamworld Theme Park. At that time, we hadn't been to any Disneyland or other giant amusement parks, and only paid occasional visits to carnivals held in west Beijing where people waited for hours to ride the Claw or other few thrill rides. I was so excited about Brisbane's Dreamworld when I first saw the brochure that we went straight to the Giant Drop the first thing after we entered the park. Jeff was not ready for such excitement in the early morning but I was quite impressed with the nice view on top and the thrilling drops. Then we rushed to the haunted house and other spins and swings. In the late afternoon we both began to feel dizzy but stayed till quite late having lots of fun.

When we flew to Cairns, the tropical town in the north of Australia, we picked up our very first rented car, a Toyota Yaris for our four-day tour there. We went on the snorkeling cruise at the Great Barrier Reef and floated on the dazzling ocean water full of colorful fish and corals in our Teletubbies-like blue diving jumpsuits so as to avoid jelly fish stings. Though smaller and cruder than the apartment in Brisbane, we loved our little cabin located in the forest, where we had our breakfasts and suppers and prepared homemade salads and sandwiches for our lunches on the way. The funny thing about driving in a left-sided traffic country like Australia was that each time when Jeff wanted to turn left or right, he would always turn on the windshield wipers. We followed the maps (literally, there was no navigator at that time), and drove to explore the wild rainforests and stunning country views. We had a total blast in Cairns!

Back in Sydney, we adapted ourselves to the city life, walking around Sydney Bridge and the Opera House, enjoying the beautiful sunshine and delicious fish & chips.

## 5. Vietnam

The trip to Vietnam in January 2008 was the last one we had before my daughter was born. I prepared for the trip after resigning from the German law firm I had been working with for almost four years and wanted to take a good rest before finding a legal counsel position. Copying my ex-colleague's travel routes, I invited two girlfriends, my high-school classmate and my ex-colleague from the accounting firm to travel with Jeff and me.

Our first stop was gloomy and cold Hanoi which didn't impress us much. We went sightseeing in the city on three wheelers. As I was well-organized and more careful about expenditures, I was "elected" to be in charge of our travel cost payments in either U.S. Dollars or Vietnamese Dong, including tickets, meals and transportation. On the train southwards from Hanoi to Hue, I couldn't reconcile my bookkeeping with the cash balance until I found out my mistake of giving a wrong denomination note (VND 100,000 instead of VND 10,000) to one of our three-wheeler drivers. The denominations of Vietnam currency notes were very high and confusing, and the three-wheeler guy wasn't honest to remind me. Jeff and my friends laughed and then comforted me that the loss was no more than RMB 30 and urged me to play poker with them.

We transited at Hue with a half-day stroll in a Buddhist temple and continued our journey southwards. The sleeping-bus from Hue to Hoi An was smelly and exhausting but when we arrived at Hoi An, we felt the trip worthwhile. Hoi An was a western style ancient town similar to the water towns around Shanghai or the old towns of Lijiang and Dali. We shopped for gifts in the artistic street stores, had the best Vietnamese spring rolls, fresh fruit juice, milkshakes and many other items of local cuisine at very affordable prices, and celebrated my birthday.

Continuing our sleeping-bus trip to Nha Trang and Dalat, we rented two motorbikes and rode them along the coastlines and in the narrow streets like local people do. Our final destination was Saigon, a modern tropical city with noisy bars and restaurants. My high-school classmate didn't like the hot weather and humidity while I was annoyed by some mean guys at the hotel. None of us had a good impression of Saigon.

After we came back, it was the Chinese Spring Festival Holiday, and I was sick with the flu. When I recovered a bit, I began to plan for a trip for late March to Netherlands with another girlfriend for tulip-viewing and visiting the "Venice of the Netherlands" Giethoorn. Then I found out about my pregnancy and had to abandon the travel plan including my hard-obtained Schengen visa.

# V

# Other Trips with Mom

After I started working and could afford better travel conditions, I made two trips with my mom, each time before joining my colleagues of the German law firm at its annual retreats. In May 2005, we took a night train to Shanghai to explore the two nearby water towns, Zhou Zhuang and Tong Li. We wandered around these two well-known water towns in southern China, visiting the well-preserved ancient residential houses, crossing various styles of stone bridges and walking on the riverside stone pavements, tasting the local food, and enjoying the quietness after the day-trip tourists left.

In the summer of 2006, I took my mom to Hong Kong and

Macau. By that time, I had been to Hong Kong several times and was familiar with the place, so I showed her around scenic spots such as the Golden Bauhinia Square, Mount Tai Ping, the Avenue of Star, and Ocean Park. On top of Mount Tai Ping, we paid a visit to Madam Tussaud's Wax Museum and took many interesting photos in one of which Mom and I stood with Jackie Cheung's wax figure. This printed photo is still attached to the TV wall of my parents' sitting room. Once a guest pointed at the photo saying that "your family photo looks really nice…"

I had done quite some research for our day tour in Macau, which was also my first visit. After we went to the Ruins of St. Paul and had a local lunch of Portuguese chicken rice and egg tarts, I even took Mom to one of the casinos to have a try. The security of the casino didn't allow us to take any food inside nor was there any storage place, so we had to finish the four Kist oranges we had just bought after lunch! Later we went to A-Ma Temple and Macau Tower. I even had a thrilling skywalk on the 233-meter-high observation deck of Macau Tower.

Mom had been to "Xin, Ma, Tai" with a tour group after retirement. She also made a few trips to cities in southern China with my father and her friends respectively. In spite of short trips to suburban Beijing during weekends, which Mom didn't enjoy much due to her car sickness sitting in our compact Golf IV for a couple of hours, it was such a pity and regret that I hadn't spent much of my free time on more trips with Mom before she was sick, as I had been occupied with my own life.

My last trip with Mom was to Gulangyu Island in Xiamen, Fujian Province, when my daughter was about one and half years old. After my daughter was born, I was obsessed with taking her to various ocean islands abroad so that she could play with sand and water while I could enjoy the sea view and go snorkeling. Gulangyu was said to be such a quiet and exquisite island without any motor vehicles, so I decided to take my mom and my mother-in-law there together with my own family. It was rather a relaxing trip when my mom, as always, took great care of my daughter and errands for me, and my daughter was such a cute doll, eager to walk around exploring everything, like animals in the zoo, a piano in the hotel and even raindrops under the hostel rooftop.

VI

# Family Trips

## 1. First Trip with Sophia

During my pregnancy and the first year after my daughter Sophia was born, I had to stay put in Beijing, despite some half-day trips to nearby parks and suburban Beijing. I missed the mountains and beaches and hoped to take my daughter out for a trip before long.

In the winter after Sophia turned one-year old, Jeff happened to have a three-day meeting at Bali Island, Indonesia, and I was thrilled to prepare for the trip for me and my baby girl. My mom warned me that I would be worn out taking care of the baby's food and sleep during the trip due to changes of places and seasons. I was not at work and still breastfeeding my daughter at that time, who was very healthy and energetic with a good appetite for rice porridge, eggs, fish, fruit and vegies. I was rather confident about being able to "handle" her because, except for the first month after she was born, I didn't use much help in looking after her, especially during the nighttime. Mom helped me during the daytime with cooking and some chores, but basically, I raised my daughter myself "by hand".

So, with our luggage full of diapers and wipers, changing pad, rice powder, toys, baby pillow and blanket, clothes for almost all seasons, hats, sunscreen cream as well as bathing suits, etc., Jeff and I started our first journey with our daughter. To avoid the potential discomfort caused by a long-distance flight, we flew to Hong Kong, stayed for one night at the airport hotel and then continued to fly on to Bali. Jeff bought seats for Sophia on the flights which was kind of a waste, but my baby girl was a bit chubby. If I kept holding her during the whole flight, my arms and legs would be really sore. As soon as the plane began to taxi and take off, I would feed her some small cookies so that she could keep chewing and her eardrums wouldn't hurt; if she began to cry, I would feed her with breastmilk and make her sleep. Luckily my daughter was coping well during the flights.

The hotel on Bali Island was fancy with nicely trimmed gardens, swimming pools and a private beach. The waiters even brought me a baby crib although we didn't know that we could reserve one when booking the room. We changed from our winter outfit to summer clothes. When Jeff went to his business meeting, I took my daughter to a waggle walk in the garden as she began to learn walking but had to lift up her arms holding my hands behind her. The organizer of the meeting considerately arranged a welcome dinner with a local-cuisine buffet and traditional dance shows for all the guests. Sophia became so excited that she kept standing up and walking around with me with my back bent forward holding her hands, which indeed made me worn out that night.

Most of the time during our stay at the hotel, I put my daughter on the beach under some shade, playing in the sand with her, or took her to the swimming pool where she wore an inflatable swimming jacket and floated in the warm water. With the long-awaited seaside sunshine and cream flowers in the tropical gardens, I felt that my happy life had come back again.

## 2. Island Trips

During the next couple of years before Sophia turned four, we took her to quite a few islands such as Jeju in South Korea, Phuket in Thailand, Hong Kong, Saipan and Cherating in Malaysia. We usually chose the winter season for our travel to the tropical places, occasionally late Fall or early Spring. Each time I did very thorough online research to find the best travel routes, compared the prices, and booked the best-deal flight tickets and hotels. In most cases, we stayed in one beach hotel for about a week enjoying the tropical sunshine, hotel facilities and brunch buffet. Sophia loved building sand castles or blowing bubbles on the beach, stepping in the sea water or playing in swimming pools. Jeff and I took turns accompanying her so the other could enjoy some solo times. At the Phuket hotel I even went snorkeling myself.

The Jeju Island trip in August 2010 was a special one and far more complicated than other island trips. First, the weather on the island was quite changeable and was mostly overcast or rainy. Second, the sightseeing places were rather scattered and our schedule was a bit tiring. We took taxies from one place to another to visit more attractions in a limited time. We went to the Teddy Bear Museum and Yeomiji Botanical Garden, saw the "stony grandpas" (Dol Hareubang) at the Folk Village and tasted black pork BBQ, hiked up the mountain ridges and craters at Sangumburi and Seongsan Ilchul-bong, experienced the lava rocks and splashing sea waves at the Jusangjeolli Cliff, played in the sand and water at Jungmun Beach. When it rained, we put Sophia in the baby trolley and covered the trolley with a transparent rain coat so that she could still see the outside. It started to drizzle when we visited Seongsan Ilchul-bong and it was rather chilly, we were a bit worried that she might catch a cold, but the Koreans were very nice and offered us abalone porridge to warm us up, Sophia was fine and energetic throughout the trip.

Another problem was the language. We hadn't been to any non-English-speaking countries before, and were indeed concerned about the communication problem. On the last day of our trip, we took a taxi heading to Yongduam Rock (Dragon Head Rock), I had to mimic the "dragon" and "head" with exaggerating gestures to make the driver understand. Later when we went for our lunch at a local restaurant, there was neither an English menu or any menu with pictures nor did the restaurant owner understand English. We wanted to have some sushi and abalone porridge. Fortunately, the customers next to our table helped us translate into Korean before paying and leaving. Then we started to receive food on our table, literally plate after plate, including fried fish, sea urchin sushi, abalone porridge, seven or eight kinds of fish sushi or some raw fish we couldn't name, as well as side dishes. We were quite nervous that the cost of the meal would be outrageous and way more than our budget. When we asked the owner to stop serving, the owner just nodded and smiled at us without saying anything. Eventually, it cost us less than an amount equivalent to RMB 400 yuan for the most satisfying and abundant raw fish meal we had ever had.

My friends always asked me if Sophia could remember any of those trips she had when she was little, I said "probably not". It might have been the same for her to play in the sand on a southeast Asian island, or at a neighboring park. Nevertheless, the getaways mean a lot to me as refreshment from my daily routines of child raising, house chores, work, and taking care of my mom after she was sick. I also believe in the power of "moments" during our family trips, which would have positive impacts on her cognitive development, because seeing the outside world could make one respectful for and compatible with Mother Nature as well as with different cultures.

## 3. Disneyland and First Trip to the U.S.

With the success of the Jeju Island trip and Sophia growing older, we started to try complex travel routes instead of staying at one place. We took Sophia to Hong Kong when she was two and to California when she was four. In both places our main goals were Disneyland, as Jeff and I had never been to any Disneyland and Sophia was obsessed with the Disney princesses and cartoon images at that time.

Having been a courageous soul when younger, I still loved riding all the spins and swings and thrill rides in my thirties. At Splash Mountain in Disney California, we were captured in a snapshot riding in a boat about to rush down into the splashing water, where I, sitting in the front, was laughing and waving my left hand like several young passengers were doing on the back seats. Sophia was nowhere to be seen with her hiding between me and Jeff, while Jeff was dodging with his head down out of instinct. We laughed about this photo for a long time.

As long as Sophia had reached the minimum height for any ride, I would take her to have a try. It was funny that as a four-year-old, she was not at all afraid of the fast speed or ups and downs of the rides and even enjoyed some thrill rides like the Thunder Mountain Railroad, California Screaming, and Grizzly River Run. Instead, she was more scared of the dark rides such as the Snow White's Adventures or the Haunted Mansion. We never had enough of the "It's A Small World" attraction and the dome-screened ride "Soaring Around the World".

Our trip to California in April 2013 was actually the first trip to the U.S. for Jeff and me. Jeff was in charge of the travel plans and bookings including the flight tickets, car rentals, hotels and all entrance tickets, and I was responsible for the daily meals and expenditure. Like many Chinese, we rushed to shopping outlets for clothes and shoes. As frugal as I have been, I got my first luxury purse at Coach. In comparison to shopping and tasting local food, we found amusement parks such as the Disneyland, California Adventures, Universal Studio, Legoland, Safari Park, and SeaWorld in San Diego more interesting. Sophia was the happiest of us, full of stamina and quite sociable playing with local kids in the parks. At Legoland, she had her face painted for less than ten minutes before going on a water slide and getting most of the painting washed off. After watching the Shamu show at SeaWorld San Diego, we got wet and it was a bit chilly in the late April afternoon. We were worried that Sophia would catch a cold and bought a huge turkey leg for her to get heat and energy. It was hilarious that the turkey leg was even bigger than Sophia's little face when she was biting.

Driving in the U.S. was much easier than in Australia, and with the navigation equipment, we felt relaxed during the whole trip. We drove all the way eastward to Las Vegas and the Grand Canyon. We were amazed about the primitiveness of the Grand Canyon; there was not a single guardrail at the edge of the cliffs! We roamed through the valleys where Sophia climbed on quite a few boulders. We even had our first helicopter tour overlooking the fabulous canyon. I had my first skywalk on a whim although the ticket price was not cheap and not included in our budget. Jeff and Sophia didn't want to try the glass floors which seemed scary, so I went up myself. I was not allowed to bring my own phone or camera, and there was a photographer taking photos for each visitor and sending them to the checkout counter for people to choose and buy separately. After finishing my tour, I came to the counter intending to see my photos but the staff member couldn't find any. He called the photographer and asked on the phone if he had transmitted the photos. When he tried to describe what I looked like, he said "…she is pretty, she is tall, uh…she is pretty tall", which tickled me and made me realize that in the U.S., I am still a tall woman.

## 4. Travel with Sophia's Friends

After Sophia went to kindergarten, her friends' parents became our friends too. It was lucky when kids played together and parents could get along well, or vice versa. As I had gained experience in arranging island trips from our previous years, I arranged two trips for four families including ours to Phuket and Bali.

The Phuket trip was the best of all. I booked a northern European-style beach hotel for three days and a boat trip to Phi Phi Island where we would stay for two days. The beach hotel was family friendly because it had many kids pools with water slides and sand-playing facilities and toys as well as kids clubs and shows. Sophia was quite at ease since she had been to some similar hotels and helped her pals (one girl and two boys, all about four years old like Sophia) to communicate with other kids or waiters in simple English. However, the first time when she was standing on one of the tall water slides, she was too nervous to slide down into the swimming pool even after her friends did so. I was standing in the pool encouraging her to have a try, otherwise, she could step aside so that other kids behind her could slide first. But she seemed paralyzed up there and just held the bars of the slide without budging. I was a bit annoyed worrying that those kids might get impatient and push her. To my greatest surprise, during the time (it felt like seven or eight minutes) before Sophia finally gathered up her courage and slid down, none of those four or five-year old foreign kids ever pushed, urged or passed over her. All those kids just stood behind her, waiting quietly. I was deeply impressed with the good manners of these kids and their families behind them.

Besides this small episode, Sophia and her friends enjoyed themselves very well. They jumped or slid into the pools to swim, played in the sand, ate ice cream, danced, drew or made art works. We parents also had a great time relaxing, taking photos, chit-chatting and enjoying delicious Thai food and fresh juices. On beautiful Phi Phi Island, we had a near-beach snorkeling half-day for both parents and kids to explore the crystalline water as well as the colorful fish and corals.

Jeff took many great photos of the four kids, with the sapphire blue sky and deep turquoise ocean as background. After we were back home, he even made a music video for each family as a happy ending of our Phuket trip. Sophia was so immersed in the memories about the trip after we watched the video that, when I called her to take a bath, she cried for about five good minutes and yelled that "I don't want to take a bath here! It's no fun here! I want to take a bath in Thailand!"

The trip to Bali was taken the following winter. We stayed in one beach hotel at Nusa Dua to enjoy the nice pools and beach, and hired a mini-bus to roam around the Kuta and Ubud areas, visiting the Holy Spring Temple, Kintamani Volcano and Ubud Palace, viewing the rice terraces and having dinner at the famous Dirty Duck. We also hired a boat for a snorkeling half-day in the outer sea, and had a sunset dinner at the famous Jimbaran Beach. When we visited the Uluwatu Temple, there was a monkey coming out of nowhere who robbed the eyeglasses of a father in our group. A vendor nearby offered to help and asked us to buy some snacks from her so that we could trade with the monkey. Finally, the father got his spectacles back, and we all felt we had been set-up by the vendor who might use the monkey as a way to sell more snacks.

The kids and parents were exactly the same as those in the Phuket trip, but the girl of Sophia's age was a bit feeble and constantly not feeling well, so her parents became quite demanding which made the rest of us quite nervous. Sophia played mostly with the two boys and the vibe became a bit sour.

It turned even worse when we were onboard at Denpasar Airport heading to Singapore for transit back to Beijing. The plane had some malfunction and we were told a few hours were needed to get it repaired. All the passengers were requested to leave the plane and stay in a large hall without any seats. We waited for the whole afternoon sitting next to some wall on the floor and the kids played cards or other games.

In the evening when there had not yet any clear instruction about the follow-up plans, we all became impatient. The girl, not as energetic as Sophia and the two boys, was sleepy and uncomfortable lying on the floor and began to weep. I felt kind of guilty towards my group of people for the poor arrangements of the airport and air company, and began to act tough in pushing the staff to take immediate action. First, we were advised to stay overnight at the airport hotel and fly the next morning, then we were told that there would be limited seats on two planes leaving for Singapore at around 8pm and 10pm so we decided to wait for any opportunities instead of going to the airport hotel. Later, I noticed some European passengers leaving the hall, so I kept asking the staff what the criteria is for people to leave at 8pm or 10pm and the issue was somehow escalated to racial discrimination. After several rounds of arguments and negotiations with the airport counter staff by me, Jeff and one boy's mom whose could also speak English, we finally got on the 10pm plane.

Later I wrote emails to the air company complaining about the malfunction and poor arrangement which tended toward bias. They got back to me with some coupons to be used on their planes, which I rejected and doubted if I would ever fly with that prestigious airline again.

## 5. Taiwan

The next spring after the Bali trip, some families of Sophia's friends decided to take a trip to Hong Kong Disneyland. Since we had been there before, we didn't join them.

I often heard that Taiwan is a good place to travel due to its beautiful scenery, delicious food and the local people being very civilized. Despite the complicated individual travel formalities, I applied for Taiwan travel permits for us and booked flight tickets via China Airlines where my high school classmate worked. We then took a one-week trip in Taiwan in mid-April, 2014, traveling from north to south, visiting Taipei, Hualien and Kenting.

We flew from Beijing to Taipei, admiring the exquisite collections in the National Palace Museum, appreciating the sparkling night view on top of Taipei 101, and having local food at the Shilin Night Market. It was fine to travel by foot or subway in the city, but when we tried to take a half-day relaxation in Yangmingshan National Park, we realized that the traffic was quite inconvenient without driving our own car (it is illegal to drive in Taiwan with a Mainland driver's license). We almost missed our train south to Hualien.

Fortunately, I had booked us group tours starting from Hualien. We joined the local tour group for a one-day trip to Qingshui Cliff, Taroko Gorge and the pebble beach at Chishingtan Scenic Area. As the schedule was a bit tight, we could only stay at each spot for a short time and could not enjoy any in-depth experience such as hiking or kayaking, but the beautiful scenery was really impressive. The next day we joined another group heading to Kenting alongside the famous Su-Hua Highway, appreciating the east coastline of Taiwan, the Tropic of Cancer Marker as well as the Pacific Ocean view.

As a five-year old kid, Sophia was pretty amazing during the long-distance road travel; she either took naps or watched outside the windows. A girl in her 20s traveling alone sat next to me in the mini-bus and kept sucking lollipops, which made me think that in the future when Sophia could travel alone, she might also have all the sweets and "unhealthy" snacks I prohibited her from having.

At the end of the bus trip, we arrived at Taiwan's south end, the coastal town of Kenting. Sophia very much enjoyed the swimming pool at the Kenting hotel which resembled the tropical hotel facilities in Phuket. We were pretty fascinated by the forest park, boardwalk at the beach, the pretty lighthouse and ocean views, as well as the night market food and souvenirs.

## 6. Russia

The trip to Russia for Sophia and me was whimsical. My ex-colleague and friend was in Moscow at that time where her husband had been dispatched to work. Her daughter was older than Sophia by a year and a half, and the two girls used to have playdates when they were toddlers. As I have always been worried about traveling to non-English speaking countries, I was more willing to go to Russia when my friend's family was there.

In mid-July of 2014, Sophia and I flew to Moscow and

stayed at a hotel close to my friend's home. Her husband drove us to the Kremlin and Red Square, where we admired the magnificent colorful domes of St. Basil's Cathedral, tried the traditional drink Kvass and tasted ice cream at GUM shopping mall. The next day my friend asked her neighbor's son, a Chinese boy studying engineering in university, to be our guide, taking us to a half-day trip through the historical Moscow Metro stations. After having lunch at the antique-styled McDonald's at the Old Arbat Walking Street and picking out gifts, we said goodbye to our young guide and took the two girls on a boat trip on the Moscow River.

On the third day, my friend borrowed bikes for the four of us to take a bike trip. We arrived at the State University of Moscow and were feeding the wild ducklings and picking up daisies when it suddenly started raining cats and dogs. We took shelter under a bus stop for about twenty minutes and until we saw sunshine coming out the dark clouds. We continued our bike trip alongside the Moscow River to the Sparrow Hills. While we were having an ice-cream break, it drizzled again. We found shelter under some trees and made up our mind to get back by cable car as soon as the rain stopped. Once the rain did stop, we changed our mind and began to push our bikes over the Sparrow Hills, when the shower came the third time. We hid ourselves under bushes and had a good laugh about our "choice and decision making" and our special cycling trip.

As my friend hadn't got any chance to travel to cities other than Moscow since she arrived, we decided to take a three-day trip to St. Petersburg by train. It was such an adventure as neither my friend nor I understood any Russian. After we got on the night train, a trainman came and said something to us in Russian. The two of us were quite confused until my friend's daughter told us in a low voice what the guy meant. Luckily most Russians can speak some English; otherwise, we would have had to seriously depend on a 7-year-old girl plus the google translator during our whole trip.

My friend compared Moscow and St. Petersburg to Beijing and Shanghai, as she felt that Moscow was a bit raw and St. Petersburg was exquisite. We appreciated the magnificent façade and glorious interior of the Baroque-style Summer Palace of Peter the Great, Tsar's Village and Catherine Palace, Winter Palace and St. Isaac's Cathedral. We also took quite a lot of pictures of the impressive Blue Bridge, Kazan Cathedral, Bronze Horseman next to the Neva River as well as the Cruiser Aurora. While we moms lingered on the brightly colored onion domes and glittering mosaic interior of the architecture, the two girls would rather spend time on playing hide and seek in the royal gardens, or splashing water on the beach at the Gulf of Finland, or just horsing around the children's playground in local parks. We even had a late supper of a traditional Russian meal at about 11pm and sauntered back to the hotel in the bright summer night.

Once finishing our exciting trip, we went back to my friend's home in Moscow and spent the last day at the children's playground in the Filevskiy Park and having an abundant BBQ picnic on the bank of Moscow River.

## 7. Second Trip to the U.S.

At the end of 2014, my beloved mom passed away after suffering from a thymic tumor for more than three years.

After I dealt with her funeral and relevant issues, Jeff booked us a short trip to the Similan islands of Thailand, on one hand helping relieve me from my agony and devastation, and on the other hand celebrating my birthday.

After we were back, my 16-year old cat Blacky died of kidney failure. I had adopted the one-month old Blacky when I was in my third year of university and he had been staying with my mom after I got married and left home. He was such great company for my mom both in life and death. I had Blacky cremated and buried next to my mom's cemetery.

I became very depressed and felt so empty that I was scared to be at my parents' house where only my step-father lived. Jeff suggested that I stay away from home and try a different environment for a change of mood. After some arrangements, we went to California for a few months in the spring of 2015, meeting friends, exploring attractions and attending business conferences and seminars.

We stayed with our friend for some time at San Jose where I felt quite relieved. During a period when Jeff had to return to Beijing for a while, my friend went to work and Sophia went to a temporary daycare, I would deal with my work, read teen novels borrowed from a local library, buy groceries from local stores, and cook American-style dinner for my friend and Sophia.

When Jeff came back, we visited friends in Palo Alto and San Francisco and drove to places we have never been to. The tech giants alongside the Infinity Loop route were neat and chic and the campus of Stanford University was massive and beautiful; I loved the chapel the most because of the blooming Jacaranda tree in front of it. In downtown San Francisco, we had a lunch at the Fisherman's Wharf and a walk inside the vintage arcade. The zigzag roads and steep streets in San Francisco were eye-opening to me, who was used to the broad and flat streets in Beijing.

We drove to see boulders at Yosemite, took strolls in the sequoia forests and stayed in a wooden cabin for the night. Stunning Lake Tahoe brought back my memory of the Lugu Lake Jeff and I had visited when we were younger. We all loved the crystal-clear water and spent a whole day next to the lake, kayaking in Emerald Bay, staring at wild geese on the beach, exploring the forest where we almost got lost, picking up giant pine cones and watching the sunset. I felt so calm to be in the middle of these forests and lakes.

Before heading back, Sophia and I went to the Disneyland in California again where we spent three days taking almost all the rides and attractions in both Disneyland and California Adventure. Sophia was so excited that she became a little chatterbox who couldn't stop talking to our American friend in English about our trip.

## 8. Qingdao Adventure

After our return to China and before Sophia started her first year of primary school, I took her to Qingdao for a three-day trip as a farewell to the summer. We took trains back and forth and visited Wusi Square and public beach by bus or on foot. We also took an hour-long bus to Mount Laoshan, famous for its majestic landscape and

Taoism myths. When we came down, I realized that we might have missed the last bus back to the downtown and decided to call a taxi.

I waited for some time watching my phone for the real-time location of the taxi accepting my order, which was very close to where Sophia and I were standing, so I called the driver's virtual number on the taxi hailing APP but he hung up on me twice. After hanging up on my calls, the driver even cancelled my order. I thought it weird and took Sophia to find the taxi based on its available plate number. The driver, a guy in his mid-40s, ignored us and my questions about the order and the phone calls. I felt insulted, swore to make a complaint to suspend his license and said angrily that beautiful Qingdao was ruined by drivers like him. After that, the driver and another guy with him were very impudent and threatened to hit me. Sophia was scared and started crying, people came around to watch and I kept calling the police emergency line, but the line was busy! Then there was a bus coming bound to the downtown, so I took Sophia to the crowded bus, leaving the driver still cursing behind us. On the bus, I sat Sophia on a platform and wrote complaint letters about the driver's behavior to the taxi hailing APP and posted it on social media addressed to the Qingdao Transportation Bureau. Several days later both parties replied me, promising to take the matter under investigation and to penalize the driver.

Afterwards, I had to reflect about my reckless behavior that, though I was bold and ready to fight for justice to the end, I shouldn't have argued harshly with those drivers when I was alone with my young daughter in a rural place, which might have put us in danger. In fact, Sophia could not remember anything about the trip other than that fight.

## 9. New Zealand

In early 2016, we planned a trip to New Zealand during Sophia's winter break to do some sightseeing and visit my university classmate as she recently moved her family there. We stayed in my friend's house in Auckland for a couple of days and hiked Mt. Eden to see the crater. As my friend's daughter was two years older than Sophia, the two girls got on well and played joyfully in the park and the beach of Torbay.

We left her family and continued our road trip in the North Island driving our rented car. Hamilton Garden was full of unique and rare flora, while Waitomo Cave was lined with light colored limestone and shining glowworms. Sleeping in the cabin of Waitomo Holiday Park was definitely a challenge for Sophia, frequently shouting at huge cockroaches and flying bugs, which in my friend's word are must-haves in "village-style" New Zealand.

Lake Taupo was massive and such a perfect place to take a break from driving, have a picnic and shop for groceries and gifts. We went to see Huka Falls, tried the Rotorua Redwood Tree Walk and hiked a bit in the lush forest. The Tamaki Maori Village show and buffet were great ways to experience the local culture, but Sophia was literally scared of the humorous Maori performer who joked about eating kids.

Before finishing our journey in the North Island, we had a great adventure of zorb globe rolling in Rotorua. Each of us tried two different tracks coming down the hills, including the twistiest, the steepest, the longest and the one with water in the globe. That was hilarious! We got soaking wet and had to change clothes before heading to the airport for the South Island.

Christchurch seemed a bit desolate and still recovering from the severe earthquake in 2011. Maybe because we stayed there for only one day in transit, the city barely left any impression on me except for the vast Botanic Garden with the colorful hydrangea flowers.

The South Island was such a treasure with a combination of all my favorite natural attractions including lakes, gardens, snow mountains, valleys, hiking routes among forests, etc. We had a picnic beside the bluish-green Lake Tekapo, visiting the lakeside church and staying up late to watch stars and constellations. We skipped stones at Lake Pukaki, appreciated large patches of lavender under Mount Cook and went hiking for about four hours in the Hooker Valley to see the crystal-clear glacier lakes.

At Queenstown, we settled into a fancy flat with a large lakeview balcony and hung out around the teal-colored Lake Wakatipu. We took a half-day cruise aboard a vintage steamship to a farm, feeding animals, having English tea and cookies and watching wool cutting. During our stay at Queenstown, we went shopping for groceries and cooked our own meals. By that time, I'd become very good at cooking western-style dishes such as spaghetti, Risoni rice, lettuce/tomato or carrot/broccoli salad, with roast chicken, minced beef burgers or steaks. Sophia has been adapted to western food since her toddler years. Therefore, such long-term overseas trips without any Chinese food were no problem for us.

The day we scheduled for the Milford Sound cruise was cloudy and chilly. After having a lakeside breakfast at Fiordland National Park, we went onboard to experience the phenomenal fjord, watching great falls and sluggish sealions lying on rocks. It was a pity that it began to rain and everything was so gloomy that the photos taken didn't have any bright colors, and we had to stay most of the time in the cabin to keep warm. Interestingly, as I haven't had a chance to take a Yangtzi River cruise to appreciate the renowned Three Gorges, this Milford Sound tour somehow reminded me of the last two lines of the great poet Li Bai's poem Departing Early from

White Emperor City, "On both banks the apes cry out repeatedly, my skiff has passed ten thousand mountains".

After visiting Arrowtown and taking our first wine tour in the Gibbston Valley, we flew back to Auckland to say goodbye to my friend's family. Sophia's biggest gain from this trip was learning to play UNO from my friend's daughter. We bought the UNO cards at a shopping mall next to Lake Taupo and had played the game wherever we had a break. We brought the game back to China and taught many friends to play. It was such a nice way for both kids and adults to stay away from the screens and have some fun time together.

## 10. The 1st Eurotrip

With Sophia growing older, to gain a better understanding about museums and foreign cultures, and with us not having thoroughly traveled to Europe (I myself had been to a few German cities and Mallorca during retreats with the German law firm), we decided to take a self-organized group trip to Europe in the summer of 2016 with Sophia's pals from kindergarten.

Jeff was in charge of the travel schedule as well as the flight and accommodation bookings for our large group, consisting of six 8-year-old kids (three girls and three boys) and nine parents (six moms and three dads). I helped with their Schengen visa applications. It was said at that time that Europe was not safe due to certain geopolitical reasons. Jeff had put Marseille into the itinerary but cancelled it at the suggestion of our friend Lisa, the mom of a boy who had joined our Phuket trip and helped me with the Bali trip flight delay. She had lived in France for years and was worried about the security in Marseille. It was funny that Jeff bought three nightsticks for our three rental cars and had each kid equipped with a cute whistle alarm. Our trip turned out to be quite safe and the Europeans we met were basically nice. Our kids were even saved by two black "uncles" from the fast closing doors of the Paris Metro.

After we arrived in Paris, Lisa and I took care of communications, ticket purchases and meal ordering. We had crepes and croissants for breakfast at a café in Republic Square and took the subway to the Champs–Elysées Avenue and the Arc de Triomphe. The happiest time for the kids was to play at the playground of Thomas Jefferson Square and the lawns of the Champ de Mars in front of the Eiffel Tower. On the second and third days we visited the enormous Louvre, the picture-like garden of Notre Dame Cathedral, as well as the palace and lakeside garden of the Chateau de Fontainebleau.

Our favorite restaurant in Paris was a chain store called Leon de Bruxelles where we had two dinners with different flavored mussels and fries. For snacks, the kids couldn't get enough ice creams while the moms enjoyed the French "Café au lait" (coffee with milk). An unhappy incident happened when we finished our tour in the Sainte Chapelle and intended to have a coffee/ice cream break before heading to Notre Dame. Our group came to a fancy restaurant at a street corner and we found seats at several tables outdoors like other customers. I raised my hand to signal a waiter who was serving drinks for other customers, but the waiter didn't look at me. I waited for about five minutes and was worried that the kids were becoming impatient and noisy, so I raised my hand again to draw attention while raising my voice saying "excuse me" but still no waiters looked in our direction. Then

I stood up and was about to enter the restaurant which seemed to be being cleaned up. A manager-like waiter stopped me at the gate and said to me very quickly, "you have to wait outside and should not come inside, this is not like your country that you can go wherever you want." I was shocked at his words and returned to my seat without saying anything.

While sitting down and waiting, I got more and more angry about the waiter's words especially about my country and told Lisa and Jeff. Lisa comforted me and expressed her compassion based on her own part-time work experience years ago that French waiters/waitresses were usually in short-supply and quite stressed and grumpy from serving so many customers, so there's no better way to deal with them than waiting quietly at the table. Soon the same waiter who had shouted at me came to our table, telling me in a moderate tone that they were extremely busy and every customer should wait at the table. I immediately retorted that, "you could have told me that over there instead of talking about my country, and if any waiter would have looked at me and let me know that they saw us, I wouldn't even have gone there!"

The guy seemed embarrassed and asked if I needed some time to order, I said "no, I can order now, otherwise our kids may get bored and disturb other customers!" He then took my order and went away. When we finished our refreshment, I was still sullen for not saying more to defend my country, but for the sake of manner and dignity, I didn't forget to pay a tip to the waiter in spite of my frugality.

Leaving Paris the next morning, we took an early train to Avignon where we picked up three rented cars and drove to the old town area. We had our late lunch, took a quick stroll to see the Palace and street shows. After the kids played on the merry-go-around and had their daily ice creams, we hit the road to Arles, taking another quick walk to see the Amphitheater and Van Gogh Café where we had our late dinner. The dusk alongside the Rhone River was gorgeous and stunning, but our schedule for that day was too tight to linger for a longer time and we had to continue our journey to Manosque that night.

The next morning, after a short swim and breakfast at the Manosque hotel, we drove to see large patches of sunflowers and lavender on our way to Valensole, the renowned lavender town where we joyfully wandered, shopped for souvenirs and lined up for the locally famous lavender ice cream.

South France is full of hidden gems. The kids swam and splashed in the water happily in St. Croix Lake and Azur Coast in Nice, and we parents were fascinated with the paving stones of the medieval village of Eze, gaily-colored flowers and deep blue ocean views. Sophia even tried a stand-up paddle board on St. Croix Lake and all the kids were crazy about the tremendous playground in Nice.

The road trip went on with more surprises. We took cable cars at Chamonix up to see Mont Blanc and went downhill to check in at an exquisitely decorated villa for the night, where each family enjoyed an independent apartment within the villa and the kids had a lot of fun playing "tag" in the gorgeous backyard. The hospitable owner, being a talented musician, showed us around the villa and gave each of us his own CD album as a gift.

Finishing our tour in Lucerne, where we stayed in the old town, went to see the UN headquarters and had a nice walk around Geneva Lake, we headed to Germany along the Rhine River. After dinner beside Titisee Lake with traditional pork shank, which quite satisfied the fathers, we followed the cell-phone navigators to our hotel in the central area of Schwarzwald, or the Black Forest. We soon realized that one of our three cars chose a different route and was separated from us. Due to the unstable internet connection in the forest region, we couldn't keep in touch with each other and became a bit worried. About one hour later, we finally managed to arrive at the hotel, and all the kids and parents were so relieved and excited that we talked and laughed at the reception, which brought complaints from other hotel guests. One dad sighed that, "What's the good of going abroad? There is not much food to eat, no way to speak Chinese, and no freedom to talk loud?" I felt the necessity to defend our group, so explained to the hotel owner that we had got separated and were excited by meeting again.

After hitting the road for more than a week, everyone became tired and some quarrels occurred among the kids. Our group split for the activities in Heidelberg where Jeff and I took Sophia to the hill-top castle and Heidelberg University as well as the old town. We stopped by the Cologne Cathedral, Roermond Outlet and Arnhem Burgers' Zoo, and finally arrived at the Giethoorn Village, the Dutch Venice I had missed out when I was pregnant. Thanks to Jeff's arrangement, my dream of visiting this serene village came true after eight years of waiting. In the drizzle, we took a stroll alongside the wandering stream in the village and appreciated the hydrangea flowers around the riverside houses.

We then visited the Gothic fairy-tale Castle de Haar and the magnificent Kinderdijk windmills, skipped the big cities like Amsterdam and Rotterdam, and drove back to Paris for their Disneyland and Outlet shopping. In comparison to the American Disneyland, one distinctive phenomenon for the Disneyland in Paris was that the best attractions on the map are mostly fancy restaurants instead of thrilling rides, which made me perceive that the French love delicious food and the Americans love adventures.

It is worth mentioning how I messed up our return trip at the airport. Maybe because I was worn out from the two-week trip and organizing a large group of people, I suddenly couldn't find the passports for my own family! Usually I would hold our three passports in hand or put them in my handbag getting ready to handle the flight check-in, but somehow I had put the passports into one of our large suitcases after dealing with the tax refund, which I totally forgot. I kept looking in my handbag and backpack, even Jeff and Sophia's backpacks. I thought I left them at the tax refund counter and someone accidentally took them away. I nearly begged the staff to broadcast an announcement but was told the broadcast department was off for the weekend. To avoid delaying others in the group, we three saw off the others and remained at the airport to see if we should contact the Chinese Embassy for new passports. Then I opened our luggage and found the passports right there! We had to check in at an airport hotel for the night and for the available flight the next morning back to Beijing. As a "well-organized" person all along, I was deeply embarrassed about the mess-up, which ruined the happy ending for our trip and Jeff's birthday on that day. Luckily the group had celebrated

Jeff's birthday the previous night in an Italian pub and restaurant where we had a blast dancing together.

## 11. Trip to the Maldives again

To celebrate my 40th birthday, we decided to go to the Maldives again, with Sophia this time.

Kurumba in the native language of the Maldives means "coconut". The welcome coconut ice cream upon our stepping onto the island was cool and delicious, but the complimentary chocolate birthday cake was even yummier. I put on my wedding dress, a red silk tank dress tailored for my wedding over a decade ago, and we took many pictures on the sunset beach.

Kurumba Island was located halfway from Male to Paradise Island to the north, where Jeff and I spent our honeymoon. Though closer to the capital city and the airport, it was still an excellent place for snorkeling. We saw dozens of colorful fish, corals and even a small shark! Sophia was a bit nervous at the sight of the shark and refused to continue snorkeling with me. She went back to the pool and I swam alone to the edge of the shallow sea and saw many sharks. I tried chasing one to watch how the shark catches prey and found a green sea turtle! I then followed the turtle and almost got stuck in the middle of the coral rocks. My left palm and foot got scratched. Luckily there was not much blood to attract any shark.

As my palm began to swell and burn, the doctor at the hotel put some ointment on my hand and prohibited me from swimming for some time. Jeff and I read on our kindles outside our room on the beach while Sophia was busy playing in the sand and sea water. Our neighbors, a German couple, asked if Sophia could play with their daughter. We agreed gladly and then the girls went to play. When we chatted, the German father expressed his amazement meeting such a quiet Chinese family as ours. He seriously asked us why Chinese people always talk so loudly, as we could hear a Chinese family of three generations not far away playing on the beach and communicating noisily. I felt a bit ashamed but Jeff explained to him patiently that in our traditional culture, people talking loudly are deemed confident and respectable, in particular in front of the elderly who may have hearing problems.

Before leaving, I couldn't help but going snorkeling the last time. I snorkeled alone to look for sea turtles and went all the way to the open sea before noticing where I was. I wasn't afraid of the emptiness at the ocean surface or the dark blue ocean trench deep down, but began to feel exhausted from swimming against the tide after snorkeling for more than an hour. After nearly another one hour, I came back to the beach totally worn out.

## 12. Kubuqi Dessert Trekking

In those years, group tours started to become diversified and "study tours" became very popular among parents and kids. Kids could be signed (alone or with parents) up for tours organized by extra-curriculum institutions to gain knowledge of biology, geology, history, etc., during the tour. We once signed Sophia up for a three-day trip with a couple of her friends when she was in the first grade to go to a nearby city for geology exploration. She was cool with the separation from us and brought back many rocks and her first lost baby tooth.

During the Labor Day Holiday of 2017, we went on a study tour trekking and camping in the Kubuqi Dessert for two days with two families of Sophia's friends. We had been camping for one night in suburban Beijing but were still worried about the troublesome and heaviness of all the camping stuff besides preparing for our first hike in the hot and dry dessert. Fortunately, the organizer provided tents, sleeping bags and pads as well as gaiters to protect our boots and ankles from sand; all we had to do was to cover our skin from sunburn and carry enough drinking water.

Walking on desert sand was really tiring, not to mention climbing over those sand dune slopes. It was sunny and bright during our two days' trekking, so we had to cover our faces and arms which made me feel a bit suffocated. I usually drink a lot of water but dared not to just in case we couldn't find any toilet or a place without being seen. Among our approx. group of 20 kids, some boys and their parents walked very fast and ahead of the line. When we arrived at some stops for a break, they had already finished their rest and began to continue walking. It seemed that we were always catching up.

Later the whole team was actually divided into several small groups, and we and Sophia's friends felt kind of relaxed staying in the middle.

Anyway, the kids were all really amazing, including 8-year-old Sophia, who completed 10 km on the first day and 15 km on the second day. During the night camping, we made a camp fire and ate watermelon while watching hundreds of stars. It would be such a relaxing night if Sophia hadn't horsed around and stepped into some puddle and I had to dry her wet boots over the bonfire for about an hour!

## 13. The 2nd Eurotrip

In the summer of 2017, we had another trip to France and Spain with Sophia's cousin Daniel and my parents-in-law. Although I felt a bit regretful about not joining the trip with Sophia's pals to Tanzania, our family trip to the lavender towns in South France and Barcelona was wonderful as well.

Arriving in Paris, we wandered around the downtown area sightseeing, as before, and visited the Luxembourg Gardens, the interior of Notre Dame, the museums of d'Orsay and Pompidou, and the Palace of Versailles that we missed out on the previous year. I was satisfied having the chance to travel with both daughter and "son" (Sophia's cousin), and quite relaxed to enjoy Paris at a slower pace, compared to the tight schedule and my stress acting as a group leader last time. Moreover, as we slowed down for the sake of my parents-in-law, we even had time to watch a theater show during the Festival d'Avignon or read books and hang out at the hotel swimming pool. At the peaceful Verdon Valley, the kids enjoyed the hotel pool as well as the water slide boat, kayak and paddleboard on the clear water of St. Croix Lake.

We took a train from Avignon to Barcelona and spent a few days tasting tapas and red sangria, watching flamingo show and hanging out on the beach. I have always been fascinated by mosaic artworks and couldn't see enough of the remarkable buildings designed by Gaudi with colorful mosaic glasses and tiles like the Casa Batllo,

Park Guell and Sagrada Familia. We blended in with local people to stroll around Rambla Street and the Boqueria Market, and had very late dinners at 9 o'clock in the evening. One month after we came back to China, we got the shocking news that a truck crashed into pedestrians along Rambla Street, the exact place we had been to, and caused devastating casualties. How I wish for less hate and more love everywhere in the world!

## 14. Trip to the U.S. Again

During Sophia's winter vacation in early 2018, we went to Hawaii. Arriving at Honolulu, we spent a couple of days on Oahu walking around the beach, shopping and visiting the Submarine Museum at Pearl Harbor. We discovered that one of Sophia's primary school classmates also came here for holidays, so we arranged a playdate and sleepover for the two girls. Though they very much enjoyed themselves by hanging out at the hotel pool and beach, having ice creams and dancing hip-hop, the two girls ended up fighting each other naked during a shower the next morning over a squabble they had!

The morning flight from Oahu to Maui had been cancelled due to the bad weather. Delayed for over an hour, we had to change our flight and landed at the east airport on Maui. After I got a taxi coupon after waiting for forty minutes for a free ride back to the originally scheduled west airport where our booked car and hotel were, we found that our luggage had been delayed too! We finished the registration for our luggage after queuing for another thirty minutes and headed to the west airport by taxi. It rained heavily on the way, and we got stuck in a traffic jam for quite some time. It was past suppertime and quite dark when we arrived. We decided not to pick up the car and went directly to check in the hotel, where the receptionist took a good ten minutes to find our booking order! After such a long day, we finally had our late dinner of some Hawaii pizza as requested by Sophia. By midnight, our luggage was finally sent to our room.

For the next days, we had a good rest at the hotel, hanging out at the swimming pool, Kaanapali Beach and the Whalers Village nearby, taking a cruise to watch humpback whales and enjoying a traditional hula dance show buffet. We also had a long day of exploration of the island, by getting up very early to take a cruise to Turtle Town, snorkeling, playing on the water slide, and watching turtles, humpback whales and fishes; in the same afternoon we drove for two hours and hiked in the Haleakala National Park to see craters and the sunset in freezingly cold wind.

During our stay in Maui, we had an interesting "accident" and were promoted for almost four hours to buy a real property timeshare. Neither of us had any idea about timeshares before, and we agreed to participate in the promotion because our hotel promised to grant us a big discount on the cost of our room. First, seven or eight couples including Jeff and I watched an intro-video together and then each sales person talked to each couple separately about the nicely decorated houses or apartments at different locations around the world. In light of the new concept of a timeshare and all the figures for down payment and installments given to us, it took me quite some time to understand the plan. We started to politely refuse the promotion as we Chinese are not so free to travel around the world as Americans are. The sales guy wouldn't budge due to the interest we had shown at the beginning and asked his manager to join in the persuasion, which made me feel even more unpleasant. Finally, since Sophia was tired of playing under the supervision of some other sales persons, and we were all starving, I grumpily rejected their lobbying so that we could leave.

Later I've learned that my middle school classmate, who has lived in San Francisco for over a decade, did invest in a timeshare apartment in Maui when his family traveled there in 2018. When Maui was badly hit by the wildfires in the summer of 2023, it was lucky that he had sold the apartment a year earlier and escaped the tragic destruction. I really hope that beautiful island recovers soon, and we will definitely visit again.

Continuing our itinerary, we took a plane a bit larger than a helicopter to the Big Island. Different from the hustle-bustle of Honolulu and the typical beach scenery in Maui, the Big Island was full of wild places for us to explore. We went to see green turtles swimming around our ankles at Hakalau Beach Park, had a sandy beach picnic at the Honaunau National Historical Park, tasted

Kona coffee at Greenwell Farms, took a bumpy Jeep ride to the Green Sand Beach, stopped by Black Sand Beach and settled at a wooden cabin close to Volcanoes National Park to see burning Kilauea Volcano in the pitch-dark night.

The hiking around Kilauea Volcano was extremely exciting and challenging. Warmed up by walking through the Lava Tube in the early morning, we hiked for nearly three hours through the solidified lava lake floor and lush rainforest along the 4-mile Kilauea Iki Trail. While having some snacks, we drove to the eastern boundary of the National Park, rode rented bikes under the bright sun for half an hour, and started our expedition across the vast lava plain to see the lava flows. There was no trail or marked route to the lava flows, so we tried to follow other hikers far and near while enjoying the dark grey shining rocks, and solidified patterns and cracks on the lava plain. As a 9-year-old girl, Sophia was my greatest pride when she completed the 4-mile tough journey full of uneven and sharp lava rocks. She only complained a bit about the hotness surrounding the slowly erupting lava at our destination. We took some nice pictures of the lava flows and headed back before it was too dark to see the rocky way.

## 15. Panda Protection in Sichuan

After the first Euro trip, we tended to have at least one trip every year with Sophia's kindergarten friends. As recommended by one mom, we went on a panda protection trip in Sichuan Province during the Dragon Boat Festival in 2018.

The three-day group trip was organized by an international volunteer trip organizer, with which I had made one solo trip for turtle conservation. The five families, including us, Sophia's three kindergarten friends and one primary school classmate, went to the Dujiangyan Panda Center, two hours' drive from Chengdu, to observe giant pandas and do volunteer work. We helped cleaning up panda dens, carrying and cutting bamboo trees, preparing panda meals with rice, corn, eggs and beans, and feeding pandas with soft bamboo shoots. To celebrate Father's Day, we also played games and did artwork. The funny part was to closely observe the pandas' poop in order to analyze their food composition. Believe it or not, their excrement didn't stink at all.

## 16. Summer Camps in the Eastern U.S.

During the summer of 2018, we went to New York for the first time. Sophia would participate in two YMCA camps in July, a two-week day camp on Long Island and a two-week sleepaway camp in upstate New York.

Before starting the camps, Sophia and I arrived in New York City (NYC) to meet up with her kindergarten friend, a girl and her mom who traveled to NYC before visiting the girl's aunt in Phoenix. The four of us hung out on Long Island near our rented apartment and went downtown for sightseeing and shopping. We pretended to give speeches at Columbia University, watched street shows and saw the huge trees in the Central Park and shopped for colorful M&M's and sweetest Hershey S'mores in Times Square. We studied plants and animals at the American Museum of Natural History, appreciated Van Gogh and Monet at the Metropolitan Museum of Art and looked out over the city from the

Top of the Rock.

The girl's mom was a great cook of both delicious and aesthetic food. I would go grocery shopping for her to cook specialties, e.g. roasted rosemary chicken or banana oatmeal pie. The girls loved all kinds of playgrounds and we moms loved taking after dinner strolls on the Long Island side of the East River, watching the NYC skyline in the dusk.

After getting suntans at Coney Island beach park, witnessing France winning the 2018 FIFA World Cup and watching Frozen, the Musical on Broadway, we said tearful goodbyes to our sisters and Sophia began her day camp. Jeff arrived and the three of us went to the Long Island dock, the iconic Empire State Building and Times Square again. We also had a day cruise to see the Statue of Liberty and Ellis Island after paying tribute to the victims at the 9/11 Memorial Plaza and fighting the crowds to take photos with the Charging Bull of Wall Street (now there seem to be fences around).

We luckily got discounted tickets for the longest-running

Broadway show "the Phantom of the Opera" and went to grab some lunch, but it occurred to us that Sophia's glasses had been left at the apartment we had newly moved into. I was worried that Sophia wouldn't be able to enjoy the famous show with her myopia, so I skipped my lunch and rushed back to the apartment to pick up her glasses while Jeff and Sophia had their lunch at Times Square. By then I was pretty much familiar with the subway lines between Long Island and downtown but it still took me quite some effort to finish the task. Fortunately, we didn't miss the show, which sadly had its final performance at Broadway in April 2023.

During the daytime when Sophia was at day camp, Jeff and I would take the subways to downtown and killed time in the public library and the MET. We once watched a street show in Central Park with a bunch of black guys "flying" over people. We rarely saw acrobatic performances by real persons (mostly we watched them in awe at the Chinese Spring Festive Gala Show) so it was quite attractive. We had been standing for about half an hour, giving two 20-dollar bills to the performers, and felt a bit fooled at last when one guy actually flew over three (selected) medium-height people instead of seven as he had claimed.

Anyway, the city life was full of variety, but we were more than happy to be immersed in nature. After sending off Sophia to the sleepaway camp at Huguenot, Jeff and I began our "wild" life as well. We headed to the West Point Museum and stayed for a week in a wooden cabin near the Catskill Mountains, where we went hiking to the grandeur of Kaaterskill Falls, trekking in drizzling rain for about 6 hours in the Indian Head Wilderness with no one else around, and canoeing on the North/South Lakes.

Jeff and I were supposed to take turns in writing emails on the camp's online account everyday so that the counsellors could print out our emails and pass them to Sophia. I wrote to her in Chinese the first day but got a reply at noon on the second day that the email system couldn't recognize Chinese characters so my email was totally illegible. At that time, we were around the North/South Lake where the signal connection was so bad that I was unable to send out a new English email until quite late of the second day. Sophia told me later that she hadn't received our emails until the third day, plus, she was too cold to sleep during the first and second nights, which almost broke her little heart, thinking that we have forgotten her!

Apart from this email accident, Sophia had a wonderful time at the camp, with full schedules of swimming, archery, canoeing, drawing and doing crafts etc. We picked her up for the weekend and sent her back for another week, while Jeff and I moved to Flushing in Queens for a week of "city" life.

The best part of the summer was to celebrate Jeff's birthday at Niagara Falls, after we were reunited and drove west. The water mist high above the falls and floating in the air could be seen miles away and was really spectacular. We've been to the Maid of the Mist, Bridal Veil and Cave of the Winds and took a boat trip in raincoats to see the great Horseshoe Falls. I hope we can someday visit the Falls again from the Canadian side.

## 17. Jingdezhen and Wuyuan

Qingming Festival is one of the solar terms of the traditional Chinese lunar calendar that falls in early April every year, when people show respect to their ancestors by sweeping their tombs and placing offerings. People also have outings to enjoy the flowers and greenery of early spring.

Though there is usually a public holiday of three consecutive days, we seldom made trips outside Beijing to avoid the crowds. We usually visited cemeteries of our deceased family members in the outskirts of Beijing and sometimes hiked for a few hours. In April 2019, we decided to join in the travel rush during Qingming Festival and to admire canola flowers in Wuyuan County, Jiangxi Province.

We flew to Jingdezhen, the Porcelain Capital of China and had a day tour in the Ancient Kiln and Folk Customs Museum, learning about ceramic clay and ancient kilns, making unglazed pottery and looking for huge bamboo shoots in the bamboo forests.

The next day, we drove our rented car to China's "most beautiful countryside" Wuyuan Scenic Area, walking around white-walled and black-roofed Huizhou-style village houses, admiring old camphor trees, rivers and bridges in southern China's old towns, appreciating large patches of canola flowers. Canola bloom season is usually in mid-March, so there are some flowers in blossom and some already with green seeds. Although our arrival was a bit late, it was actually a good season to pick fresh tea leaves. We then perfectly combined our hiking tours with spring tea picking. It was such a nice short trip!

## 18. Tibet

In the summer of 2019, we finally made our first trip to Tibet with our Phuket and European travel mates, the two families of Sophia's kindergarten friends.

Stepping out of the airplane cabin at the Lhasa Airport, I immediately felt my faster heartbeats and felt like walking on soft carpets. Ten-year-old Sophia and her pals were fine reacting to an altitude of approximately 3000 meters above sea level, but everyone was reminded by the driver and guide that we should not eat too much for the supper, nor drink any tea or alcohol or take showers on the first night.

The next morning, we drove to Nyingchi to enjoy the bluish green Lake of Basumtso and the lush Lulang Forest at relatively low altitude areas. Although the weather was cloudy, the large patches of bright yellow canola flowers and green grass under the snow mountains were quite amazing scenery. On our way, we took quick shots in the freezing wind at Mila Mountain Pass and Segrila Pass, 5013m. and 4728m. above sea level respectively, and ran back to our van to catch our breath.

Following the Brahmaputra (Yarlung Tsangpo) River, we headed to the mysterious lake Lhamo Latso, the holiest lake in Tibet where in legends people could see their past and future lives from the lake surface. True or not we had no idea, but we were ready to challenge ourselves with high-altitude hiking above 5000 meters. The way to the mountain top viewpoint was up about 300 meters of stone steps, dotted with barren rocks and pretty colorful blossoms. One of the boys walked rather fast so I caught up with him just in case he needed anything, leaving Sophia with Jeff and the rest of the team behind. Thanks to the continuous physical exercise, I was fine walking upward at a normal speed and had the extra energy to squat down taking photos of those little flowers blooming in the cold. It took about 40 minutes for all of us to arrive at the lookout where we saw the grey hoof-shaped lake far down in a valley surrounded by mountains. I tried my best to stare at the lake for any vision about my past and next life but could barely perceive anything. Perhaps it was the gloomy weather or my not being devout enough, but the mirror of the lake didn't show me any sign. We joked for a while, appreciated the lake and then took some photos before walking down. The mom of the boy who arrived first tried to walk with her son and walked so fast that she began to feel sick back in the van and didn't have any supper. The rest of us were fine with only a bit headache.

The day when we arrived at the Samye Monastery happened to be May 15 on the Tibetan calendar, the annual Universal Prayer Day. We joined the local Tibetans and queued up under the hot sun for about two hours to enter into the splendidly decorated Samye Temple, being touched in the heads by the Rinpoche (living buddha) and tasted a small portion of blessed food and drink. It was such luck and a blessing for travelers! We also visited the Yumbulagang Palace, the first palace built in Tibet, also Songtsen Gampo and Princess Wencheng's summer palace before moving the capital to Lhasa.

The following trip to Shigatse became tougher because of the higher altitudes. We walked by the turquoise water of the sacred Yamdrok Lake and admired the Karola Glacier located at 5000m. above sea level. On our way to the Everest Base Camp, we passed many snow mountains including the world's third highest peak, Kanchanjunga at the border of China and India.

It was drizzling in the evening when we arrived at the Everest Base Camp. Sophia and her pals were socializing with some local kids, while Jeff and other parents were settling at the tent for the night. I explored around alone, checking the Rongbuk Monastery and the monument to Mt. Everest elevation measurement with "Altitude

8844.43 Meters" (recently updated to 8848.86 Meters) inscribed on the monument. Later when the rain stopped and the sun came out, the whole team walked to the monument area admiring glorious Mt. Everest at sunset.

Despite high-altitude sickness, cold outside and primitive accommodation inside our tent, we had a memorable time at the base camp. Jeff and the other dad cooked delicious instance noodles with vegetables for supper, then we played cards and told jokes together. Besides the inner part consisting of a crude kitchen and the host's bedroom, the tent hall was mainly occupied by a huge L-shaped "Kang" (earthen bed) where all eight of us slept side by side for the night. It was quite noisy and cold during the night as the host's relatives kept coming in and out of the tent, plus the quilts and pillows smelled, so most of us had a sleepless night and got up very early to wait for the sunrise. Jeff and I walked out and each found a small mound shielding each of us from the freezing wind for about nearly an hour. The waiting and coldness paid off when we witnessed the marvelous moment with golden lines of dawn surrounding Mt. Everest!

We then visited the Tashi Lhunpo Monastery in the rain and headed north to Yambajan. Heavenly Lake Namtso at 4718m. above sea level definitely amazed us with its purity and holiness. Sophia and I put on our bright-colored dresses and took great photos between the pure skies and waters.

Back in Lhasa, we felt very relaxed as if we were back at sea level (actually an altitude of around 3500m.) and started drinking beer with delicious Tibetan food to celebrate our almost-finished tour. We visited the colossal Potala Palace and the sacred Jokhang Temple in the hustle bustle of Bharkor Street. The must-see outdoor live show of Princess Wencheng was such a great combination of historical storytelling as well as legendary dance and music that both parents and kids were excited to be fully engaged for about two hours till midnight.

## 19. National Holiday Trip to Yunnan

During the 70th National Holiday of the country, we flew to Yunnan. Our original plan was to transfer at Kunming airport for Xishuangbanna, but due to the change of flight schedule, we spent a half day wandering around Dianchi Lake and the Yunnan Ethnic Village. Years ago, Jeff and I had been to Dianchi Lake but weirdly neither of us had any impression of the vast green lake. Sophia was more interested in the traditional food and snacks in the Ethnic Village so we spent most of our time there having a feast and watching folk cultural shows.

It was my first time in Xishuangbanna, a border city with an exotic south-eastern Asian style. The Tropical Botanical Garden was huge and full of gorgeous foreign species of flowers, fruits, trees and cacti. Walking under the bright blue sky and among the humid rainforest plants reminded us of some zoos in foreign countries. Wild Elephant Valley with various orchids, butterflies and tropical plants was also a nice place for hiking, but we were not lucky to see any wild elephants during our trip.

We even met some long-time-no-see friends there and our two families had great chats and ate local cuisine together. Later we strolled in the Starlight Night Market on the Lancang River bank, hunting for pretty necklaces and incense candles. Sophia got her hair braided with colorful threads as she always wished. Besides, the Dai Show was definitely a feast for the eyes, especially the breathtaking "hair hang" acrobatic dance and the touching story of the Peacock Princess.

Our next stop, Dali, was also a place of memories. In contrast to the smelly night bus and our backpacking trip more than ten years ago, even our early flight was not much of a problem. We picked up our rented car and drove around the vast, clear Lake Erhai, the "Pearl of the Plateau". Later, to complete our trip of the "Jade Erhai and Silver Cangshan", we rode the cable halfway up to the Cangshan Mountains. Sophia saw a funny thing on the way up in the cable car. One "pawn" on the giant stone Chinese chessboard was wrongly placed as it was not supposed to go backwards.

When we were hiking in the mountains, it suddenly started to rain heavily. We held up my shawl under a pine tree for about ten minutes and then decided to run downhill with some other travelers instead of waiting for the rain to stop. It was quite slippery and the rain kept falling, and the three of us all became soaking wet and started to feel chilly. The weird thing was, when we arrived at the foot of the mountain, the ground was pretty dry and it seemed no rain had fallen at all! We then bought some grilled purple potato and sausages to warm up and changed our wet clothes in the car.

Jeff and I had been to the old town of Lijiang years ago, so we decided to stay in Shuhe Old Town for a change. There were pubs, restaurants and souvenir stores alongside the river that meandered throughout the old town, but Shuhe was much quieter than Lijiang during the night. For the sake of time, we didn't go to Jade Dragon Snow Mountain, but drove to Tiger Leaping Gorge to see the rushing river of the Golden Sands. We all love to spend time staying in our picturesque hostel and walking around the cafes and stores in the old town.

# VII

# Solo Trips

## 1. Nepal, 2014

My solo trips were not actually "solo", but traveling with female friends other than my own family as a change. Ever since my first solo trip to Hainan in 1999, my life had been fully occupied with work, exams, my daily routine, as well as taking care of my mom and my daughter; therefore, I didn't have any chance to travel on my own or with other friends until 2014 when I finally decided to leave my 6-year-old daughter with Jeff and take a 12-day trip hiking in Nepal with two female friends, my ex-colleague and her ex-colleague, to see the great snowcapped Annapurna and other Himalayan peaks.

We had planned to follow the 5-day Poon Hill loop trail that my other ex-colleagues, also three ladies, had taken in the previous year. However, when we arrived at Kathmandu, the trekking guide and porter we engaged told us there would be a public holiday after our 5-day hike when most famous scenic spots would be closed, and then we wouldn't be able to look around the temples and pagodas in Kathmandu as scheduled. Therefore, we decided to shorten our trekking tour to 4 days.

Leaving the hustle and bustle in Kathmandu, we took a shabby bus filled with local people to Pokhara, the starting point for all the trekking routes nearby. We stayed there for one and a half days and went boating on pretty and tranquil Fewa Lake in the late afternoon when heavy rains suddenly poured down and we got soaking wet. We met several Chinese trekkers coming from Tibet. At that time, it came to me that trekkers need to have their laundry done during the trip so that they would have clean clothes to wear and look "decent" even after being on the road for more than a month. While my previous trips didn't last such long time, and I hadn't been caught up in such a situation when the clothes for change were not enough.

Compared to other trekking routes to the Everest Base Camp, our counter-clockwise Poon Hill tour was said to be a "baby" (moderate) trek, and most trekkers would take 3 or 4 days to finish it. As we were female beginners, a 5-day tour would have been more suitable and relaxing. To shorten it to four, the second day would be very tiring as we were supposed to trek about 14 kilometers from Ghandruk to Ghorepani, the village near the Poon Hill mountaintop so that on the third morning we could go to see the spectacular sunrise over the Annapurna Himalayan range. And that was so true! Though the porter carried most of our heavy clothes and washbags in his backpack, I was carrying Jeff's solid Canon 5D-Mark II camera and wearing a pair of heavy trekking shoes, and I was the only mom and not as young as my friends, so I was still exhausted from the non-stop climbing on the second day. I took a lot of breaks as my heart and lungs needed air, and the guide/porter was a bit annoyed and worried that we couldn't arrive at the hotel as planned before darkness. Anyway, we made it after more than 7 hours of walking through the thick jungles and climbing up endless stone steps with heavy moss; we reached our hotel.

In the early morning of the third day, we got up when it was cold and dark at 4:30am, and climbed steps for an hour to the Poon Hill viewpoint. Luckily, we saw the starry night sky, the color-changing of dawn and the splendid sunrise above the snowy mountains. When we went back to the hotel, we had our lavish breakfast in front of the fascinating snow-capped Fish Tail!

The tour down during the next two days was much easier in spite of the countless stone steps and the poor living conditions in the guesthouses. When we finally got back to Pokhara, we rewarded ourselves with great food and drinks at the TripAdvisor-recommended restaurants and even had our first tattoos! One of my friends had an elephant tattoo on her left shoulder blade and the other had a small black cat on the back of her ear and "Eyes of Buddha" on the back of her waist. I had an infinite loop on my left upper arm. The only pity was that we were unable to take a paraglider due to the rainy weather but I later chose to take a sailplane over Pokhara and took many nice photos with my cellphone.

Back at Kathmandu, we went to the renowned Monkey Temple near Durbar Square and other places in the old town. Later in 2015 the whole place was heavily destroyed by a strong earthquake and had to be rebuilt. We even went rafting in some suburbs but the floating was not as thrilling as expected. Moreover, due to our new tattoos, we couldn't jump into the river to have a good swim.

In a nutshell, the Nepal trip was a breakthrough for my life. I wish I could take a similar trek tour someday while I am still able to make it.

## 2. Krabi, Thailand, 2015

With the successful experience in Nepal, on Christmas of the following year, I went on a 6-day snorkeling trip at Krabi, Thailand with my ex-colleague, who came there from Munich, Germany.

I love snorkeling in the sea ever since I did it for the first time in Maldives, and I have been to Thailand many times with my family, mostly in Phuket Island and once in Similan. But this was the first time I went without my family and the first time to Krabi and Lanta Islands. I had a great time with my ex-colleague, an independent and outspoken Beijing girl who could speak fluent German and some English. We went sightseeing in a minivan and a long-tail boat, enjoyed food at a night market as well as at fancy beach restaurants, rode scooters around Koh Lanta in the rain, and saw many pretty fish and corals while snorkeling. I accidentally touched a purple sea urchin and my finger got badly swollen.

Later I went back home, and my friend continued her journey for another week to take cooking lessons. At that time, she had not yet married her German boyfriend and still worked hard at developing her career. Currently, she has two lovely daughters at her new home built in Stockholm, Sweden where her husband was dispatched from Germany. How I miss those sisters' trips when we were all wild and carefree.

## 3. Pilgrim tour to India and Nepal, 2016

After my mom passed away at the end of 2014, I was in

deep grief for a very long time. I didn't stop my travels, though, which I needed more than ever to help myself get over the devastation and loss in my life. When my friend Lisa asked me to join her and her friends, a devoted Buddhist couple whom she called "big brother" and "big sister", to worship buddhas in India and Nepal, I agreed immediately.

I had been longing for a journey to India, a country with an ancient civilization and the famous Taj Mahal, but was concerned about the safety and hygiene issues during self-arranged trips. Traveling with friends in a group of people on set schedules was a perfect choice. Furthermore, I became curious about Buddhism or other religions like the Christianity, for their religious "power" to possibly cure my grief and loss from my mom's passing away. After preparing for the trip for about a month, including previewing some Buddhist sutras and even reciting a long paragraph of the "Peace" Sutra, I took my third "solo" trip before Christmas of 2016.

The trip was very lighthearted, as the tour group (the young Chinese guide happened to be the son-in-law of

Lisa's "big brother") had everything organized from our visas, flights, hotels and meals, to the local transportation and admission tickets, except that during the whole 12-day trip we would have to eat vegetarian food as Buddhists do. I am not a meat-lover, so I had confidence about adapting to the food. It turned out that I became very fond of desserts and fried food in the last few days of the trip, due perhaps to the lack of meat or fish for more than a week.

It was indeed a heart purifying trip. When my friend and I joined dozens of other Buddhists in the group to walk around the Buddhist pagodas or stupas for seven (or less but always an odd number) circles or sit cross-legged on the ground in front of temples or buddha sculptures, reading the sutras loudly. I guess when we concentrate enough on doing one thing, no matter what that thing is, we feel inner peace and tranquility.

Something weirdly interesting happened when we were wandering in the ruins of the renowned Buddhist Nalanda University. I somehow became popular like a celebrity attracting local Indians, especially guys taking photos with me. Maybe it was because of my outstanding height as an Asian, or my appearance (wouldn't deny about my attraction in spite of age). Whenever our group stood somewhere waiting for our bus or entering the tour stops, there were always some Indian guys staring at me, talking among themselves and then coming shyly to ask to take photos with me. Lisa and other group members started to joke about me being the "appearance representative" (in Chinese "Yan Zhi Dan Dang") of the group.

The pilgrim trip was eye-opening in spite of the polluted air in the rural places and the contaminated water of the Ganges River of India. I was fascinated by the Red Fort in Agra, as well as the Taj Mahal mausoleum that was built by the emperor Shah Jahan for his favorite wife. I was deeply impressed by the dedication of the Buddhists in the group, including their generous donations and devout behaviors such as reciting and chanting prayers and sutras, lighting batches of candles in the Bodhgaya Temple very early in the morning, hanging prayer flags in many high places, and mostly importantly, the touching "Long Kowtow", when they put their bodies on the ground and stretch their whole bodies as long as they can, then stand up with both hands together, all the way up to the Vulture Peak along the Buddha's meditation route. Nevertheless, I was still unable to persuade myself to believe in Buddhism. As Lisa's "big brother" said, it is not yet the "right" time for me.

## 4. Sea turtle protection in Sri-Lanka, 2017

I had been following a WeChat official account of a volunteer trip organizer, which introduced different travel routes at home and abroad for travelers to do volunteer work such as animal protection, trash collection, senior care or school teaching in rural places rather than only sightseeing. I thought such trips would be more meaningful and chose the sea turtle protection program in Sri Lanka as my fourth year's solo trip.

My friend Lisa had some days of unused annual leave and agreed to join me in the 6-day trip starting from late November. We flew to Colombo and took a car locally rented for us by the trip organizer to Galle, an old costal town in south-western region of Sri Lanka. The work at the sea turtle care center had been arranged in the mornings, which included cleaning up the sea turtle tanks, carrying buckets of sand from the beach nearby, preparing raw fish for the turtles and taking care of sick turtles and soft turtle eggs, like ping-pang balls. We met two foreigners from Europe on the second day at the center, and we picked up trash on the beach together. In the afternoons, we paid an extra fee to the driver so that he could take us to the old town and some scenic spots nearby, enjoying our free time and local cuisines.

It was said that November might be a good time for whale watching but we were not lucky due to the early coming of the rainy season. On the fourth day it started to rain heavily. When we went back to the hostel from our morning work, the power in the whole village was out because of the rain. Our hostel was not far from the sea, and we could see the splashing waves from our room on the third floor. After we ate quite a few snacks and drank local beer in the candle and torch light (no supper was prepared due to the lack of electricity), Lisa casually mentioned that we may need to flee the hostel in the middle of the night if the sea waves got stronger and turned out to be a tsunami coming all the way to the village. I was startled as I had never thought the rain could be so disastrous. While I started to panic, Lisa went to sleep on our double bed. I silently packed a small bag with my phone, passport, wallet and a bottle of water, and thought about the clothes I should wear if we had to flee in the midnight, before falling into sleep, too.

The next morning the rain stopped. Although the power outage was still ongoing, we were no longer worried. On the way to the sea turtle center, the driver told us that many people standing on the beach were actually waiting for the bodies of their family members who had gone fishing in the previous days. We were as gloomy as the weather, and worked even harder to clean up the yard of the sea turtle center after the thunderstorm.

There was an old French lady who had been staying on the second floor of our hostel for nearly a month in Galle. When we chatted, she told me about her trips to Myanmar, Cambodia and other places in Sri Lanka, while I also shared my travel experience from my trips in Nepal, India, Vietnam and so on. She was surprised and admired me as "such a great traveler".

## 5. Italy, 2018

A friend of mine went to Milan in late 2017 to study Italian and look for business and immigration opportunities, so I decided to visit her in the early spring of 2018 and the two of us could have a sisters' tour in Sicily. I had not been very close to this friend nor had I known her character much except for some previous work-related connections. She had been self-employed in Beijing for many years and was not financially well off. That said, I was still astonished when I saw her sharing a small twin-bed room with an Italian girl, with a third Chinese girl staying in a separate room of an apartment where the three of them shared the bathroom, kitchen and public area. I could totally relate to her ideas about saving money and was fine having my own hotel room in Milan, visiting the Milan Cathedral on my own and paying our first supper when she forgot to bring enough cash or credit card, as long as we could have a great trip together in Sicily.

However, everything seemed to go against us. Firstly, we forgot to do online check-ins in advance for our flight from Milan to Catania and arrived late at the boarding gate, so we missed our flight. We were both worried about our original schedule being delayed and wasting the hotel we booked in Catania, and we tried to reason with the airline staff to find any potential solution. But I admitted inwardly that it was our omission about the online check-in and the late show-up, so I didn't argue harshly. My friend was mad about the airline staff and me. She acted like all these Italians were bullying us out of racial bias or discrimination, while I as a lawyer didn't try my best to fight for our legitimate rights. The good thing was that she could yell her anger out on the phone at a service staff member of the Chinese travel agency, which had actually oversold the flight tickets leading to the unavailability of our seats. In the end, we had to stay at the airport hotel and fly the next morning. We got all the fees including the supper costs covered by the travel agency. I felt satisfied with the negotiation results and intended to move on. My friend seemed to hold a grudge and acted strangely, blaming me for putting a heavy bag of food on the floor and standing next to a trash bin. On the first evening we shared the hotel room, she left the toilet floor wet and slippery and her used tissues and towels everywhere after taking a shower. I began to feel ominous about taking the trip with her.

Catania was a nice Baroque city on the east coast of Sicily, and was much warmer and cozier than cold and rainy Milan. The room we booked was in a residential building where we could use the kitchen to cook our own meals. The landlord was so nice that he didn't charge us for the previous night when we were unable to show up due to the flight issue. I was talking to the landlord about the special places nearby when my friend urged me away. She said the landlord was very nagging and my conversation with him was such a waste of time. I said the landlord was just showing his hospitality, when my friend retorted ironically that, "How could you become a lawyer if you cannot tell the difference between nagging and showing hospitality?" I didn't want to argue with her and remained silent.

We booked a day trip to Mt. Etna Volcano and arrived early in the morning at the bus stop after buying some pizza for lunch. I suggested we take the front seats for the two hours' drive to avoid carsickness on the hillside roads, but my friend couldn't bear the smelly guys around us and insisted on sitting at the back. I went with her. After half an hour, my friend got carsick and staggered forward. Since there was no vacant seat, she had to stand next to the driver, covering her mouth and looking pained. As soon as the driver stopped for a break and opened the front door, she rushed out to find a tree to throw up. I brought her some water and waited for her to recover.

Fortunately, she felt better on the second half of the journey. Arriving at the foot of Etna, we got off the bus and my friend started to shiver in the cold mountain air. She said she was too cold and weak to go around and had to stay in the coffee shop next to the bus station. Therefore, I continued the tour on my own. I spent about an hour hiking around Monti Silvestri and the other crater near the parking lot, picking up some volcanic rocks and taking some selfies of me sitting on the edge of the windy craters. I met some travelers from our bus and they all asked about my friend. It was still early for the return bus, and I definitely wanted to make the best use of the day trip. I then started to walk up the mountain. I hiked on the sandy earth road for half an hour under the warm sun and found a shelter to eat my pizza lunch.

As I went up higher and higher, the road became icy and slippery. With my Converse sneakers and crossbody bag, I was neither mentally prepared nor physically equipped for climbing a snow-covered mountain. Nevertheless, I am not a quitter. In light of my earlier hiking experiences and my confidence about my own strength, I continued to walk steadily and carefully. Two hours later I was exhausted and cold, feeling that my T-shirt inside my sweater and winter jacket were sweaty. The wind was strong and it was very gloomy and foggy, I couldn't see the proper way upwards or hear other people around. I was a bit desperate. What if I got lost on the mountain? There was even no phone signal or network connection - how could I call for help? While thinking wildly, I heard someone talking and I yelled "hello" excitedly. A Polish couple who were skiing downhill encouraged me, saying I was only ten minutes away from the cable station. When I finally arrived at the store and the cable station, I had a small bottle of fruit liquor to warm myself up, and took the lift down.

My friend was not interested in the routine tour of seeing as many attractions as possible that I usually did, so the next day we went on separated tours in the ancient town of Catania. I strolled for a couple of hours to the Catania Cathedral, the Roman Theatre and other must-see places along Church Street. Later my friend and I converged to walk to Ursino Castle and the fish market, where we had a fancy lunch of fried fish and ink pasta before heading to Palermo.

Palermo was more historical than the dynamic Catania and looked more like the traditional Italian town in the classic movie "the Godfather". We roamed around the Cathedral, Norman Palace, Fountains of Pretoria, Quattro Canti and so on. At a souvenir kiosk my friend was intrigued by the lovely magnetics on the display board and checked them closely. I was standing outside and reminded her to be careful with the broad sleeve of her coat touching the magnetics. Unfortunately, one magnetic was knocked down on the ground and broken in half. When she tried to bargain with the owner for the broken magnetic from 5 euros to 1 euro and was refused, she started to raise her voice claiming the magnetics weren't worth 5 euros and the owner was blackmailing her. I was speechless and walked away.

After several hours' walk, I felt my legs were sore and wanted to find some food at a restaurant around the Massimo Theatre. My friend insisted on looking for a "special" restaurant for dinner so we wandered for another hour until finding one place satisfying to her.

I have become quite sociable through the past years' traveling abroad, as I always believe most people in the world are kind. My friend obviously held the opposite opinion. Our Bed and Breakfast at Palermo had a kitchen and dining area for residents to cook their own meals. I met a young couple in the kitchen traveling from France and chatted with them happily. Back in our room, I was in a great mood sharing with my friend that the neighboring girl came from Taiwan and her French husband was a writer when my friend warned me that the couple didn't look nice and it was weird to spend a month in one place writing something. I was silent again and for the first time wished our journey could end soon.

Finishing our tour in Sicily, we flew northwards to Rome. My friend said she had been to most attractions there and wanted to meet friends in the city, so I took a solo tour again and agreed to join her for dinner. Despite the drizzling weather in Rome, it took me the whole afternoon to saunter around the Colosseum, Arch of Constantine, Palatine Hill, Roman Forum, having a quick look at the Bocca Della Verità without entering, wandering around Piazza Venezia, Trevi Fountain and the Spanish Steps. It was a pity that the Pantheon was closed when I reached there. I was too weary to go back to eat with my friend, so I sent her a message and enjoyed pasta with fish and white wine on my own.

The following day I took the subway to the Vatican Museum, St. Angelo Castle, Vatican City and the Sistine Chapel. I stood in the chilly rain for about two hours to enter into the Vatican Museum and my shoes were wet. Maybe because I had waited for so long, the Vatican collections didn't amaze me much, whilst I was rather impressed by the tranquility in the yard of St. Angelo Castle as well as the river view nearby. I had a happy-hour drink and some snacks at a local bar and took the bus back.

In Florence, I also did most of my tour on foot alone. I spent the first day exploring in the old town area, ambling around Florence's Santa Maria Cathedral, Santa Margherita Church, Uffizi Art Museum and the old bridge. In the late afternoon I climbed to the top of the Cathedral's dome to enjoy an extraordinary view of the old town and listen to the bells ringing in the chilly Florence spring. On the next day I went early to visit the Accademia Gallery for Michelangelo's statue of David, walking through the Church of Santa Cross as in the film "Da Vinci Code" and even sauntered across the Arno River to the hills outside the ancient city area to overlook the skyline with Florence Cathedral and other iconic architecture in town.

Returning to Milan, I felt rather relieved to go back to the hotel I had stayed at one week ago. Surprised to find China's bike sharing service "MoBike" there, I cycled around the city area by bike and on foot and felt good about being called "Bella" (beauty) in a local park. As recommended by my friend, I took the train and went on a boat trip on Lake Como. However, due to my "greedy" arrangement to walk around the gardens and villas at

Bellagio, I almost missed the last train back to Milan. Interestingly, when I was running from the dock to the train station and stopped at the intersection panting, I saw some other girls running there too. I asked one of them if they were catching the train to Milan. They said yes, so when the traffic light turned green, we ran along together.

Out of respect, I wanted to have the last supper in Italy with my friend before leaving, and she wanted to cook at her apartment instead of dining out. After a whole day's trip from Como, I was weary and wished to shop quickly, but my friend had no idea about what to eat and was very selective. I suggested cooking noodle soup with eggs and vegies and making some salad, she agreed but insisted on going to another store to buy eggs. I became a bit indignant and followed her on foot for another ten minutes to buy eggs before going back to her home.

My Milan trip was the last solo trip I had before the Covid-19 pandemic outbreak. I had planned to visit Czechia, Austria and Hungary with a female friend in March 2020 but had to give it up due to the spreading virus and lockdowns around the world.

# Recent Family Trips

## 1. Tokyo Skiing Trip

Our last family trip before the pandemic was a skiing trip in Japan in early 2020 with a group of "pro" skiers. By that time, the three of us had mastered certain skills to ski well on all beginner's slopes and some intermediate trails at the snow resorts in suburban Beijing. Sophia and Jeff attended a couple of training classes. Sophia, with the help of her ice-skating techniques, could make good parallel turns. While I didn't take any class and would rather go at my own pace, after years of falls and crashes, I was able to slow down on most moderate slopes or make wedge turns at a low speed.

Our friends' group, consisting of six teens and their parents, had spent most of their time in winter going skiing home and abroad, and become quite good at skiing on both resort trails and wild snow slopes. I decided to join them to improve our skills and to have our maiden trip to Japan (we hadn't been to Japan due to language and timing issues). We almost had to give up the trip due to the more and more intense situation in Beijing after the pandemic outbreak in Wuhan, but managed to "escape" from Beijing before a potential lockdown. Moreover, we were able to bring back facial masks for our extended families and friends in China, which were in urgent need during the early stage of the pandemic.

It was rainy on the first night of our arrival at Hakuba Valley, the Japanese Alps and three hours from downtown Tokyo, so the next morning the snow in lower areas of the snow resorts was melting with exposed soil, and therefore not suitable for skiing. After breakfast we put on our own clumsy ski boots and carrying our ski boards (newly purchased for this trip), we took three shuttle buses to the Happo One Resorts, which, according to our group leader who's my friend's husband and obsessed with powder snow and back-country skiing, was a "proper" place for us.

Pretty soon I began to realize what a big mistake I had made by being overconfident. The medium level trail at Happo One was unexpectedly hard and I couldn't control my speed as in the Beijing resorts. Neither could Jeff. Under the foggy and cloudy sky, Jeff and I tumbled innumerable times skiing down the slope and could barely ski for ten meters! Sophia was just fine catching up with the rest of the group heading to the trails on top of the mountain, with my friend and another mom taking care of her. Jeff and I were left alone struggling to practice slowdowns and making turns on the massive slope. I can clearly remember how awkward we looked when we kept falling in the snow with hoodies and pockets of our jackets filled with snow and our legs and hips extremely sore.

Later that evening, we soaked ourselves in the hot spring waters at our hotel and had body massages in the massage chairs outside the hot spring area, we felt refreshed and our tense and sore muscles relaxed. Luckily our legs were strong from years of stair climbing and hiking, and we "survived" the first day of our skiing trip.

For the rest of the days, we didn't join our skillful friends to challenge ourselves. Instead, we chose the snow resorts around our hotel so that we could practice on easy or intermediate trails based on our own levels and rhythms. Sophia decided to stay with us because she still had lingering fears about having to ski down the narrow slopes on the top of the mountain on the first day. We all loved the Tsugaike Snow Resort the best for its winding and smooth mountain trail for beginners. The snow-covered forests alongside the trails were very pretty. The Norikura Snow Resort was right behind our hotel and was convenient and time-saving. After five days of continuous practice, our skills had been greatly improved and we seldom fell down while making turns at controlled speeds. I appreciated my friend for taking us on this trip, perfectly paring skiing with hot spring soaking.

There was a heavy snow on the third day. The snow on some upper and lower parts of the trails could be as deep as 30 to 40 cm. Sophia liked to sit or lie on the snowy ground making giant snowballs or snow angels. We tried different cable routes to explore almost all the beginner and intermediate trails in Tsugaike and took many amazing photos with the blue sky and white snow as backgrounds. But one father in our group had his ankle broken while skiing in the deep snow and the family had to terminate the trip earlier than planned. I felt fortunate that we could be safe and sound despite the first day's risky challenge.

We spent the last two days of the trip roaming in downtown Tokyo, drawing lots at the Sensoji Temple, buying lovely Lucky Cat souvenirs and visiting the Museum of Nature and Science, Edo-Tokyo Museum and the Sumo Museum. Most importantly, we managed to buy masks and some other cosmetics while tasting the local eel rice, sukiyaki (beef hot pot) and sushi go-around.

## 2. Domestic Trips during Pandemic

The pandemic didn't actually lock us down at home for

a long time, except that I had to cancel my previously booked trip to Eastern Europe in March, 2020. Jeff and I worked from home and Sophia took online classes during the weekdays, on weekends we went hiking in different parks in the city and suburban areas and even traveled out of town a few times.

### 2.1 RV Tour to the Meadow

In the summer of 2020, we rented a recreational vehicle and drove to the Mulan Paddock, the royal hunting area of the Qing Dynasty, with our friend Lisa's family. Our van was rather small, suitable for two to three people while Lisa's was larger for four to five. Although I was able to stand straight inside the RV, ours was still crowded for the three of us to stay in or sleep.

Jeff and I took turns to drive the RV while Sophia mostly stayed in Lisa's RV, playing cards or video games with Lisa's son and Lisa's parents. Driving an RV was almost as easy as driving a normal car as long as one would be careful of any height limit and obstacles when making turns.

When we arrived at our campsite in Chengde, Hebei Province, the rain had stopped and it was pitch dark. In the lights of both RVs, we had a self-served BBQ dinner between the parallel RVs. Due to our omission to close the door each time we got out of the RV, there were tons of bugs and mosquitos inside. We fought and drove them out for half an hour and spent another hour taking showers in the tiny leaky bathroom and unfolding the extra bed under the dining table, before finally settling into sleep.

It was bright and sunny the next day. We went walking around the lake and valley in the Saihanba National Forest Park, experiencing tranquility in the midst of white birches and wild flowers as there were not many tourists during the pandemic. Then the kids and fathers went boating in a beautiful lake, while we moms enjoyed our self-served coffee and chit-chat in the serene lakeside campsite.

Our final destination was the Ulan Butong Grassland in Inner Mongolia, where we rode in a horse cart to explore the massive prairie, dotted with colorful blossoms and clear lagoons. Sophia was very brave to ride a large horse by herself and played happily with her pal.

Back from this trip, Sophia started her study and life in a prestigious middle school. With the nationwide pandemic under control, we took the chance of the National Holiday "Golden Week" in October to climb Mountain Tai, watching the sunrise and commemorating my trip with Mom decades ago. Then we took the train to visit Jeff's 97-year-old grandpa in another city.

### 2.2 Enshi, Hubei

During the Labor Day Holiday of 2021, as recommended by my friend, a mom of Sophia's kindergarten girlfriend, we joined a study tour heading to the Enshi Grand Canyon in Hubei Province. We hadn't traveled with tour groups for many years but I had to admit that, a well-organized study tour brought us a lot of carefree fun.

About 13 kids were divided into three teams to complete missions such as taking photos of landmark scenery inside the canyon and looking for special shapes of limestone to earn points, and the team arriving earliest at the exit would be the winner. We parents followed our kids, took photos of them at designated places while enjoying the magnificent cliffs and valleys at the same time. The competition turned out to be a bit intense, and for most parts of the tour we had to walk fast or run to catch up with the kids. One mom older than the others had to rent a sedan chair carried by two men to save effort of climbing the stairs. In the end, Sophia's team was the second one to arrive but earned the highest score. Both kids and parents got along well after this half-day ice breaking program.

The next day, we went whitewater rafting in the Tangya River. Sophia and I were on one inflatable raft while Jeff shared one with a father in the group. At first the river was so shallow that we almost got stuck in rock shallows so Sophia jumped into the water and dragged our boat to the deeper water. Sometimes when the current was fast or we were going against the stream, we had to row very hard with the paddles. What a perfect arrangement to have our upper bodies exercised after the previous day's hiking exercising our legs! That said, our hard work was worthwhile because the gorges were enchanting with steep cliffs and lush plants, and the river was clear and green.

There are many minority ethnic groups in Enshi Tujia and Miao Autonomous Prefecture, and we stayed in a quiet village of the Qiang ethnic group. The kids on a team basis went to the bamboo forest to cut bamboo canes. Then each team carried one bamboo cane of about five meters long back to the village, sawed it into 20cm long sections and put sticky rice into the tubes to cook for dinner. The steamed rice in the bamboo tubes smelled fresh and tasted delicious. We also helped villagers to pick tea leaves and went on a hike in the fresh mountain air after a rain, looking for hidden waterfalls.

On the last day of our tour, each of the three teams were given a big job to interview local kids and villagers about the village history and local lifestyle, and also to invite local kids to our dinner and bonfire party held in the courtyard of our two-story bamboo building. Our kids helped to make dumplings and exchanged gifts with local kids. Everyone had a blast dancing and singing around the bonfire.

## 2.3 Classmate Trip to the Grasslands

During the summer of 2021, some of Sophia's middle school classmates planned a trip to the grasslands of Inner Mongolia. I had booked a volunteer trip to Qinghai and Gansu but decided to delay it for the sake of Sophia's classmates' trip.

We drove from Beijing to Ulanqab, "the top of the red cliff" in Mongolian. Sophia and her classmates rode horses, went grass sliding and played soccer, practiced archery and played on a giant see-saw under the blue sky with large flocks of white clouds. The second day, we visited the Yellow Flower Valley, a part of the best grasslands around Hohhot filled with grass, rocks and wild blossoms. The extinct volcano clusters looked like the moon's surface and reminded me of the craters at Mt. Etna in Italy I had been to.

Sophia shared her hotel room with two girls for the nights and spent most of her time hanging out with her classmates. The girls partied every night after I took away their cell phones, eating snacks, watching reality shows and chit-chatting in bed. They accidently stained the white sheet with chili oil. The hotel threatened to charge 200 yuan for the sheet and the girls panicked. I purchased them a bottle of bleach at 10 yuan and they managed to soak and clean the stain.

With the teens more independent, we parents could enjoy our time having the lamb hot pot, local steam buns and drinks. Unfortunately, Jeff had to go back early to check on my father, who hadn't covered well from his neck surgery a month before.

For the last two days, although a bit distracted by my father's condition, I still enjoyed the momentum of the trip being with my girl and other teens. We went rafting in a mountain stream and laughed with tears during the bumpy downhill ride in an off-road vehicle. We went to another volcano relic and climbed the rocks with hands and feet. The Chahar Culture Museum and the Jining Battle Memorial Hall were quite educational, and I even found an old photo of my grandfather's brother-in-law commanding at the battlefield back in the 1940s!

Coming back from the trip, I had to cancel the following volunteer trip as my father's status was not stable. With the pandemic situation more and more severe, we couldn't make any travel plans for the coming winter vacation.

### 2.4 Beach Trip in Sanya and Volunteer Trip in Qinghai and Gansu

My first time to take a flight was from Beijing to Shanghai for a company training two months after my graduation from university. Since then, I have traveled by air at home or abroad at least twice a year, except for the year of my pregnancy. However, I hadn't flown since the Tokyo skiing trip in early 2020 because of my father's difficulty with mobility after two surgeries, Sophia's busy schedule with middle school studies and the stringent pandemic control measures.

I was about to break down and decided to try to catch a glimpse of hope as soon as I could. After almost a half year's frequent nucleic acid tests and lockdowns, the policy finally eased up in early July 2022. As soon as

Sophia commenced her summer vacation, we left Beijing for our two-week journey.

Together with my mother-in-law, we flew to Hainan Island where Jeff's brother and sister-in-law arranged an amazing tropical island tour for us. Staying in a fancy hotel with a buffet breakfast that had a wide variety of food, beautiful gardens and nice outdoor pools, we took almost all of the thrill rides and drops in a waterpark, and visited an ocean park with sea animals and shows. We also went shopping at outlets, eating homemade seafood cooked by my sister-in-law and riding shared scooters after dinner, etc. I got excited and a bit carried away, losing my Ray Ban sunglasses and snorkeling goggles when I was flipped over by the big waves in Sanya.

Waving goodbyes to Sophia's cousins' family, my mother-in-law and Jeff, Sophia and I continued our volunteer tour to Qinghai and Gansu Provinces. Because of the unexpected pandemic lockdowns throughout the country, I had been much worried that the volunteer tour I paid for last year would be cancelled. Luckily despite some cancelled or delayed flights and the nucleic acid tests nearly every day, we accomplished a wonderful tour of "Qinghai and Gansu Grand Circle", admiring the vast yellow canola flower fields in the foothills of the Qilian Mountains, riding a rope fixed hot air balloon to see the multicolored landforms against the sunset at Zhangye Danxia National Geological Park, visiting the marvelous Mogao Grottos, riding camels on the Echoing-Sand Mountain, walking on the mirror-like white or clear turquoise lake beds at Emerald Lake and Chaka Salt Lake, and riding horses next to enormous, sacred Qinghai Lake.

In light of the nature of our "volunteer tour", we had assignments such as planting trees, protecting deserts and picking up trash at different scenic spots. To gain a better understanding of the historical cultures around the areas of the Hexi Corridor and the Silk Road, we learned "Ebru painting", an art of paper marbling from ancient Asia, to draw on the water surface by shaking or dipping oil-based dyes and print our own drawings on souvenir fans or notebooks. We also learned to make bamboo slips of the Han Dynasty, writing traditional Chinese poems on bamboo slips with writing brushes and linking the slips together with threads.

Our tour group consisted of some teens and a young couple who were humorous and smart. Working, studying and hanging out with them made me feel refreshed and energetic, almost back to my 20s. Moreover, I was really fascinated about the history and art works of the Mogao Grottos after our visit there and watching the indoor scene-experience drama, "See Dunhuang Again". When I came back to Beijing, I started binge listening to a podcast about Dunhuang, to make up for regret about our short visit to only a few of the Dunhuang caves.

## 2.5 Skiing Trip in Chongli

By January 2023, almost all the pandemic control measures in the country had been removed. Though most people were worried about the contagious virus and would rather stay put during the winter season, we decided to go out of town for a skiing trip while celebrating the Chinese Spring Festival and my birthday.

At that time, our intermediate-level skills were stable, and we wanted to challenge ourselves on the more professional skiing trails in Chongli, Hebei Province, a place that is a three-hour drive from Beijing and is where China successfully held the 2022 Winter Olympic Games.

The hotel suite Jeff booked was warm and spacious, and the skiing trails around the hotel were long with snow-pines scenery. Although it was much colder than the coldest winter in Beijing, we felt great to be able to explore most of the intermediate and advanced trails with very steep slopes, until the second afternoon, when I got stuck in a large area of moguls, those horrible steamed bun like snow bumps.

The mogul trailhead was marked "intermediate" and seemed fine for us, but when we found the moguls it was too late to return. While Jeff and Sophia barely managed to make the turns among the snow bumps, I freaked out. I took off my skis and decided to walk horizontally to another trail, but after trying a good ten minutes, I ended up being stuck in even deeper snow in a patch of wild pine trees. I had to ski back to the trail and made each turn very slowly. It took me about half an hour to finish the mogul area after falling down twice. Being exhausted, sweaty and cold, I became furious and humiliated when meeting Jeff and Sophia again. I even got mad at them for (Jeff's) choosing that trail and (both) "ditching" me alone up there.

Other than this incident and after my anger died down, we pretty much enjoyed our rare getaway after the past few months' lockdowns. We tasted different cuisines at the nearby restaurants, played video games in our room and even had a hot-pot dinner with a friend's family who also came skiing.

## 3. East U.S. Again

Five years after our last visit to the United States, we had another trip to New York, Boston and Vermont during the summer of 2023.

With the international travel policies simplified, we booked round-trip flights, rented a car, arranged accommodations as well as Sophia's two summer camps as early as April. However, changes always run faster than plans. It occurred to us in late June that Sophia's middle school graduation ceremony would be held on the day after we set off. Sophia was very upset about missing the ceremony. I certainly felt for her but meantime was worried about the changed schedule and additional costs, as we planned to fly with Sophia's kindergarten friend, whose mom couldn't accompany her to the summer camp. After my negotiations with the school leaders failed and as advised by my friend Lisa, I reluctantly changed Sophia's own flight so that the schedule for the rest of us remained unchanged, the flight-cost loss was less and Sophia could join us at New York's Kennedy Airport after participating in the graduation ceremony in Beijing.

Thanks to Lisa's help and Sophia's independence and courage, everything went smoothly and our delayed meeting was accomplished. In Boston, we had a nice city walk from Fenway Park all the way to Cambridge and even had casual tours in the campuses of Harvard and MIT. In the late afternoon after Sophia finished her day camp for marine biology research, we hiked around some beautiful lakes and ponds. On Saturday, we drove to Walden Pond that I long dreamed of ever since I read both Chinese and English versions of Walden by Thoreau. We hiked a loop in the serene woods and a wonderful picnic next to the emerald green pond.

During the second week after Sophia departed for her five-day trekking expedition in the Adirondack Mountain Reserve, Jeff and I made our first visit to the State of Vermont, hanging around old town bookstores and cafés in Arlington and Burlington, buying maple syrup and of course, hiking trails at Mount Equinox, Green Mountain National Forest, Causeway and so on. Two days before we were to pick up our daughter, we left Vermont, and went on the Charlotte Ferry to New York State. To pay tribute to Sophia's ongoing trekking around Mount Marcy and Lower Wolfjaw Mountain, Jeff and I took a 16-kilometer hike from Rooster Comb up to Lower Wolfjaw. Similar to the Catskill Mountains five years ago, it took us almost seven hours to finish the "out and back" muddy and buggy trail in the quiet mountains. Our friends later asked whether we were worried about wild bears in the woods, I denied this and said our concern was basically focused on refraining from stepping in the mud and locating the "Trail" tags on tree trunks. Thankfully we hadn't become wasted during the prior three years. Although our legs were too sore to walk without wood sticks for the last phase downhill, we accomplished our mission.

The last week we came back to New York City. Times Square was bustling and dazzling as usual, and Sophia was excited to go back to her favorite M&M and Hershey's stores. I, on the other hand, was accustomed to a less crowded environment and overwhelmed by the hustle and bustle, and even got a bit sick and dizzy. We went to Central Park to find some peace and had dinner at Applebee's, one of the few times we dined out during our whole trip, as we mostly shopped for groceries and cooked our own meals.

I am truly grateful that the pandemic has been nearly over and we could travel freely again. I sincerely hope to continue my footsteps over every inch of this lovely planet, Mother Earth.

www.ingramcontent.com/pod-product-compliance
Lightning Source LLC
Chambersburg PA
CBHW030302130626
46549CB00002B/652